Every Little Breeze...

Louise Hutton

Published by Yerman Press

First published in the Republic of Ireland by Yerman Press 2001.
First edition.

A catalogue record for this book is available from the British Library.

ISBN 0 9540458 0 7

Printed and bound in the Republic of Ireland by
Ross Print Services, Greystones, County Wicklow.

Louise

Every little breeze seems to whisper "Louise"
Birds in the trees seem to twitter "Louise"
Each little rose tells me it knows
I love you, love you

Excerpt from *Louise*, performed by Maurice Chevalier, in his 1929 debut film, *Innocents of Paris*.

Contents

Sugarloaf Mountain

As I rushed down the Dublin road
On a dark and squally day,
I slowed when Sugarloaf came into view
Such beauty on display.

The clearcut silvery pointed peak
Spotlighted by morning sun,
Cushioned by misty hills and shaped
By energy now long gone.

If I could rise to the peak of my powers
And focus in like fashion,
The varied facets of my life
Could feed my new-found passion.

Writing to be good requires
The utmost dedication -
The mountain soaring high provides
The needed inspiration.

One of my general publicity theatre photographs (1948).

Introduction

I woke up this morning with the same thought I wake with every day - I'm still alive! Surprising when I think back to my earliest memory, all of eighty-six years ago.

I have been asked what started me writing. Actually, I can't remember. It wasn't to do with any specific happening. I think that it was because I had, and continue to have, my own ending in sight. I will soon be in my nineties. I needed to know, as we all do, where I was going, and had my life brought me any nearer to knowing? I found it difficult to remember many events and so I started writing them down. Certainly I was writing before my old friend, Sydney Stokes, introduced me to the group with whom I still meet every Thursday morning. They encouraged me very much, and still do, to write down all I remember of those ninety years and assured me that many more memories would come back if I did so. They were right.

When I was born in 1911, who would ever have imagined that we were going to have two World Wars to cope with, and also a rebellion in Ireland which would eventually free most of our country from British domination. My family had always wanted Home Rule, but within the British Empire. They were opposed to violence, no matter who committed it for whatever reason. However, when it came down to it they supported Britain whenever she was under threat. During the First World War, my mother entertained wounded soldiers who had been sent home from the Western Front. She took them out into the countryside for picnics. Later, during the Second World War she flew the "Union Jack" from a pole in the garden. Despite the mixed feelings in Ireland about the war, nobody ever bothered her or told her to take it down.

I used to write a diary at one time which taught me to condense my prose, and the Thursday writing group has been very complimentary about my style of writing. Now I have completed all the main stories, and I have chosen many attractive photographs which help to illustrate them. I have included the key events in my life, from my early memories of Easter 1916, to playing hockey for Ireland, to acting on stage with Mícheál MacLiammoir, to working in London during "the Blitz", to running my own puppet theatre, to coming home and buying a farm and, finally, to getting married - almost in spite of myself. I believe that there will be something in here for everyone.

In my opinion, I have been badly treated by some of the publishers that I approached. They seemed to take forever considering my material, and then they would avoid making a decision one way or the other. So late last year my son and I decided to "do it ourselves", in association with a local printer of our acquaintance.

Thank you, Peter, for all the time and effort you put into selecting and adapting so many beautiful photographs, and for the much appreciated editing of all the writing. Thanks also to Patrick Gallagher of the Bray Writers Group, who gave us his picture of Sugarloaf Mountain, specially painted for the cover. Finally, thank you to David Wheatley for his kind words.

I believe that this book proves that "you're never too old to start". If you feel that you have something to say, or do, you shouldn't be put off by those people who tell you that it will be too difficult. You can achieve anything if you put your mind to it. Of course, this book has been difficult, and it would never have been finished without the hard work and support of my family. I am proud of what we have managed to achieve together - I hope that you enjoy it.

Louise Hutton

March 2001

Huttons

I belong to a family who used to live in the middle of Dublin, where they made horse-drawn carriages. They developed a significant reputation for these carriages over a period of 146 years.

In 1779, John Hutton founded the firm in small premises at 63 Great Britain Street (now Parnell Street). Ten years later it moved to larger premises at 115 Summerhill. When his friends told him that he would lose business by moving so far away from the city centre, he replied that if his carriages were any good then his customers would follow him - and so it transpired.

In the early 1790s, Hutton commissioned Rudolph Ackerman to design a series of carriages for him. The latter belonged to a German coach-building family, and he had been working in London for many years producing designs for many of the large coachbuilders there. Subsequently, he produced a series of designs for John Hutton and Sons, some of which are reproduced in this book.

Funnily enough, I never travelled in a horse-drawn carriage when I was young. Years later I was surprised to discover how light and springy it felt, in comparison to the solid motor cars in which we drive around today. It had to be light enough for one horse to pull. It's easy to forget about the poor old horse and all the food he would have consumed. Add to that, each horse would have been unique with a different character. I'm sure that ours would have had good dispositions as we would have loved them so much.

People didn't realise how much work went into preparing the inside of the carriages. Cushions had to be made to fit and to match the curtains. To start with, Huttons sub-contracted this work to Messrs. Fry and Sons of Westmoreland Street. After moving to

A Hutton touring car, built in the 1850s.

Summerhill, they had additional space and so were able to take on this work themselves. They also created a separate department to keep records of the coats of arms of their aristocratic customers - these were usually painted on the carriage doors.

The coats of arms would have been painted by hand, of course.

John Hutton and Sons employed up to 160 men in the second half of the nineteenth century. When Queen Victoria visited Ireland in 1837, she travelled from Kingstown (now Dún Laoghaire) in a comfortable carriage made by the firm. She enjoyed the experience so much that she ordered one just like it for her herself. This Hutton carriage is still in use by the British Royal Family. It is called the Irish State Coach, and it is used by the Queen every time she opens Parliament. I've actually seen it in action.

After some unscrupulous competitors started to copy their designs, Huttons decided to brand all their work.

A cousin of mine used to be a member of the Atheneum club in Lower Regent Street, in London. One year, she arranged for us to go to this club on the day of the official opening of Parliament. We watched on television as the coach started out from the Royal Mews in Buckingham Palace. Then we had just enough time to run down the steps to see the coach pass down The Mall towards Admiralty Gate, around the corner of Trafalgar Square and on to Westminster. Then we retreated again to the Atheneum, and watched the entire service at Westminster on the television. We felt very special as we watched "our coach" taking such a central role in the proceedings, although we knew that it had been almost completely renewed in 1911 (the year I was born) after being largely destroyed by fire.

The twentieth century brought a long list of new challenges and these would combine, in the end, to bring down John Hutton and Sons. At first, they adapted very well to the changing circumstances. They brought some of the first motor cars into Ireland, and they appointed Dr. Colohan - the first Irish motorist - onto the Board of Directors. However, not all of their decisions were wise ones. They should still have been trading today if it hadn't been for the innate snobbery of one of the Hutton directors. He turned down an offer from the Ford Motor Company to be their agent in Ireland. Huttons had already been appointed the agent for Daimler, and he thought that the two lines wouldn't mix! However, the Ford models were cheap to produce and popular with the public, and the decision to turn down the franchise was a critical factor in the subsequent demise of the firm.

The early 1920s were troublesome years for Ireland and her people. As a consequence of the War of Independence, and the ensuing Civil War, most of the potential buyers of the Daimler - the landed gentry - left the country in large numbers. Huttons struggled on for a few years, taking in repairs and selling what cars it could. In the end, the firm found that it could not sustain itself in the new economic environment, and John Hutton and Sons went into voluntary liquidation in 1925. The premises at Summerhill were sold off to the Dublin United Tramway Company, and they exist today as a depot for Dublin Bus.

Baron de Caters tries out the latest model, Summerhill, Dublin (1903).

Our family has a number of other claims to fame. A brother of John Hutton, called Henry, held a number of high offices at the turn of the nineteenth century. First he was an Alderman of Dublin. Then in 1792 he was appointed High Sheriff and, in 1803, Lord Mayor of Dublin. He built and lived in a large house overlooking Dundrum called Wyckham Park, which survives to this day.

John's eldest son, Robert, was Liberal MP for Dublin during the 1830s and 1840s. In the 1837 General Election, he was elected along with Daniel O'Connell in the two seat constituency. Robert came a very close second, polling 3,542 votes or only 14 fewer than O'Connell!! I've often wondered what would have happened if Robert had achieved a swing of just eight votes - would the main thoroughfare outside the GPO have been named Hutton Street? Somehow, I doubt it.

Our final claim to fame comes from Annie Hutton, who was the daughter of John Hutton's second son, Thomas. In 1843, she and Thomas Davis met and fell in love with each other. Annie was only eighteen and he was twenty nine. There is a theory that they were introduced to each other by Frederick Burton, a painter who was a mutual friend of both families. A reproduction of one of his paintings of Annie and her two sisters appears later in this book.

A few years earlier, Davis had been one of the founders of the "Young Irelanders". These were a group of young men who published articles encouraging Ireland to throw off the yoke of British rule. They even advocated active resistance. My family had always supported Home Rule, but only if it could be achieved without the use of violence. So, to start with, they considered Davis to be thoroughly unsuitable and wouldn't allow him to court Annie. To make matters worse, he had given up his job as a barrister to take up politics and, as a result, he had no money to support a wife. In 1844, Annie's parents sent her away to stay with relatives in the hope that she would give him up. However, he continued to write many letters and poems to his beloved Annie, and she reciprocated with some delightful letters.

In due course Annie's family relented and, in 1845, Annie Hutton and Thomas Davis became betrothed to be married. Sadly, barely a month afterwards he died from scarlatina. Naturally, Annie was heartbroken. Some time earlier, Davis had asked her to undertake, on his behalf, a translation of Rinuccini's "Embassy In Ireland", an important source of Irish history. For several years thereafter she continued to work on this, even travelling to Italy with her mother in order to carry out some related research. However, she was destined never to complete the work.

In June 1853, Annie died of a broken heart, having never really recovered from the shock of her lover's death. She was only 28 years old.

My parents - Thomas Noel Hutton and Alice May Hutton (née Robertson), and my brother Wilfred (1903).

Beginnings

I was born in 1911, in number 29, Upper Pembroke Street, Dublin. It was one of the tall Georgian houses, with wide granite steps leading up to the hall-doors and attractive fanlights, much beloved of today's postcard makers. I have to admit that I don't really like Georgian architecture which makes these streetscapes like narrow brick canyons, with no visible roofs to break the monotony. Oh yes, I appreciate the fanlights and balconies now, but I wasn't really aware of them when I was living there. I do remember the basements, however, with separate outside steps leading down into "the Area" where the tradesmen's entrance was. This was forbidden territory for me. I also remember the many storeys above ground, with only two rooms on each floor. Take away the house on either side and one was living in a veritable tower with ten flights of stairs from top to bottom. My two brothers used to tear up and down these stairs at high speeds, doing two steps at a time, and I did my best to emulate them, improving my "times" as my legs grew longer.

On one occasion, I caught my wrist in the banisters as I turned the corner about halfway down. It was quite painful and I sat down and started to cry hoping that someone would come and comfort me. But nobody came. They were probably too far away to hear me. I tried to keep on and on crying until someone would arrive, but in the end I had to give up. I remember clearly the feeling of frustration and loneliness as I continued on down, without the loving sympathy I craved.

There must have been four storeys in our house, but I can only remember three. The study first, with two walls lined with books. I loved it and I could often be found curled up in an armchair deep in a book. But if my father was sitting behind his desk it meant business, and little girls were hardly welcome.

The dining-room was towards the rear and I don't remember it in detail. Being small I hardly ever ate in it. But there was a very intriguing small lift there which was wound up and down by hand. It brought up dishes from the kitchen, and carried them down again when the folks above had been served. I loved to be at the operating end below in the kitchen, and then to run upstairs to see if it had arrived safely.

My brother Walter and me outside 29 Upper Pembroke Street, Dublin (1915). The house is now part of the Dublin Institute of Technology.

Above came the two drawing-rooms, front and back, with folding doors between which could be opened on special occasions to make one big room. I have a picture in my mind of the lightness and brightness of these rooms with the white marble fireplaces and the elegant furniture, all lit by the tall Georgian windows by day and the beautiful chandeliers by night. They fascinated me, these chandeliers, especially when once a year they were taken down to be washed with soap and water and laid out on towels to dry. Then they were reassembled, which was quite a task! Sometimes I was allowed to help by handing the now shining, three-sided crystal-like pieces, in the right order, up to my mother standing on the step-ladder for her to hang them in their right places. The chandeliers had been electrified and tiny flame-shaped bulbs lit them up instead of candles.

I can still see my father in his comfy chair by the fire, with his drink beside him, reading the newspaper. This was kept carefully folded for him until he got back home by tram, after working all day in the Dublin office of Brooks Thomas. He would be tired and rather "tetchy" and wouldn't want much to do with a small daughter at that moment.

On the next floor was the "master" bedroom, and the spare bedroom behind. I had a special affinity for the latter with its high double bed. When I was about three my Scottish Uncle Bill came to stay, and I fell in love with him and used to climb into his bed each morning as soon as I was let. I can still feel his comforting warmth and his kindness. Much later I learned that Uncle Bill was considered the "Black Sheep" of his Scottish family, and was inclined to borrow money which he couldn't repay. I'm glad I didn't know or care about that at the time, and only knew that I loved to be with him.

There were also times when I climbed into my parents' bed, such as early in the morning on Christmas Day. I kept warm in between them while opening my Christmas stocking. My two brothers, five and ten years older than me respectively, were allowed to tuck in at the bottom. We all had stockings, even my mother and father. As I got older, I remember well their excitement and enjoyment as they opened all the strange assortment of things we had collected and packed into theirs.

Wilfred, Walter and me
in Fitzwilliam Square (1917).

A less happy occasion was when my father was in bed with a

cold. My mother was making a dress for me, and she brought me up to her bedroom to try it on. I was never easy to fit as I couldn't bear to stand still for long. I got more and more fidgety, and my mother more and more exasperated. She was nearly in tears, and we had both forgotten all about my father, when suddenly there was a roar from the bed 'Stand still, ye little so-and-so, and let your mother fit ye!' My fright was such that I froze, and my mother was able to put the pins in. But I never forgot that moment and held it against my father for a long, long time!

My parents and two brothers on a picnic in Poulaphouca, County Wicklow (1913). I must have been left safely on dry land!

Up another two flights must have been my nursery where my nurse and I slept, and the boys' room at the back, but I have no memory of these rooms at all. Strange! You would think that I'd remember my own room above all, but I don't. I much preferred to be in the basement. In the kitchen where Lizzie Fitzgerald, our cook, presided. She was one of my favourite people.

The Kitchen

My earliest memory is of falling down the kitchen stairs at the age of two and a half! I can clearly remember the awful moment when I reached for the banister at the head of the dark stairs - and missed! After that, all is confused as I went head over heels right down to the bottom. I'm told I sat up and roared as my nurse ran down after me to pick me up. Lizzie, although much nearer, just threw her apron over her head and wailed like a banshee. She believed that I must be dead, although thinking about it she must have heard me howling loud enough to wake the dead she thought I'd joined!

I have a very unclear picture of the big flag-stoned kitchen, which was very dimly lit by the one window out to "the Area", as it was called. A large, old-fashioned black range took up all of one side. This was fed from the mysterious coal cellar which extended out under the front steps of the house. It was filled through a coal-hole built into the pavement above. The range kept the kitchen lovely and warm, but its warmth was no greater than Lizzie's welcome and that of Mary the parlourmaid, Kate my nurse and Mrs. Mulligan the charwoman. She came once a week and scrubbed everything scrubbable. She it was who polished "the lino" at the top of those dangerous kitchen stairs, where I would often stop to feed the mice.

The door to the long narrow yard was there and I loved to pick tiny, cupped ivy leaves that served to hold water or breadcrumbs, which I would then put down for the mice behind the store cupboards or in any tiny nook or cranny. Don't ask me why - I think I was sorry for them, or maybe it was the instinct which makes other children want to have a doll's tea-party. I never liked dolls. Anyway, when I got down to Lizzie, she would enquire how the mice were. When Mrs. Mulligan ventured to say, 'Miss Louise, you shouldn't be feeding them mice - they're only pests!' Lizzie would reply, 'Ah now, hold yer whisht, Mrs. M. It's you that has the place so clean up there, that they're starvin' for a bit to ate!' Lizzie understood full well that Mrs. Mulligan never cleaned behind things - only the bits that showed.

Lizzie was a real country-woman with a great sense of humour which she could express with a natural dry wit that never failed to charm. She loved children, and always seemed to have potatoes on the boil, and would mash one with butter and salt and put it on a saucer for me. She would take me on her knee at the fire and sing me a song, of which she had a great repertoire. One of my favourites was "The Little Beggarman" which had plenty of verses. If I had a cold, she would sing:

'Oh my love, it's a cold ye've got,
Come into the bed and I'll make ye hot.'

I wish I could remember the rest of the lines. It's difficult to believe now, looking back, that Lizzie stayed with my family for over fifty years, only getting home to Carlow for her one fortnight's holiday each summer. I'm sure my love of kitchens in general started in Lizzie's.

But one problem arose in connection with Mrs. Mulligan. I must have asked, as all children do, where I came from. Someone, I suspect it was my nurse, told me the charwoman brought me! I had accepted this for years, but later on when I was about eight or nine, it suddenly dawned on me that I didn't belong to the Hutton family at all! I was devastated and miserable for days. I can remember the sick feeling in my stomach. Then someone, I think it was my mother, reassured me that she and Daddy were my real parents and I got happy again. But it took all that time, eight or nine years, before I became aware of myself, and who I really was.

I never remember my mother in the kitchen at all, though she must have descended there each morning to decide on the menu for the day. At that time of day I would probably have been out for a walk with my nurse. When I grew bigger, I would be taken to play in nearby Fitzwilliam Square with the privileged children of the neighbourhood. You had to live round the square or in adjoining streets to have a key to the gate. I wished we hadn't one because the other children all seemed older than me and were inclined to be bossy. We usually played "Camps" which necessitated joining one camp and trying to take prisoners from the other. I was always taken prisoner and made to sit under a bush in the enemy camp afraid to move and shaking with fright. On one such occasion when I arrived home again in tears, my mother was so angry that, taking me by the hand, she marched me back again and confronted the other children. She told them in no uncertain terms what she thought of them! Result - I was never asked to play "Camps" again, which I suppose was a relief, but they jeered at me instead, calling out:

'Tell-tale Tit,
Your tongue shall be split,
And all the little dogs
Shall have a little bit!'

With hindsight I know that my mother handled it badly. It was my nurse who should have been told off. She was sitting chatting to another nurse, quite happy as long as I was with the other children. But now I felt an outcast and never made a friend there that I can remember. Later on when my nurse had gone, my mother found me very difficult on occasions. If she met a friend and wanted to introduce me, I would go silent and refuse to say 'Good-morning' or indeed anything! I became known for this, and one week-end when I was about five I went with my parents to "The Island" Golf Course at Malahide. To get to this course we had to take a short trip in a boat which lasted about ten minutes.

My father tries to show me how to swim, much to my apparent discomfort, Malahide (1915). However, later on I seem to have recovered.

On this particular day a friend of my parents called Tommy Hughes, who was considered to be a wizard with children, set himself to get me talking. I resisted all his overtures and remained obstinately silent. As we reached the other side, he made one more effort and said 'Well Louise, and what do you think of me?' I opened my mouth for the first time and said very firmly - 'ROTTEN!' and everybody laughed at poor Tommy's discomfiture.

We all loved "The Island" in spite of its inadequate clubhouse, and I was allowed to go out on the course with my parents as long as I remained "good" and didn't disturb their play. I could wander along in the "rough" which grew the most beautiful carpet of miniature wild roses and violas, and other wild seaside flowers, that I had ever seen. Sometimes I would help to retrieve lost balls, which were hard to distinguish whenever the white and pink roses were in bloom. Other times my father took great pleasure in helping me to bathe off the little sandy beach, before we settled down to eat our picnic lunch. It was that kind of unspoilt idyllic place.

It actually comes into my story much earlier, on Easter Monday 1916.

1916 And All That

I was only four years old when the rebellion of 1916 broke out but I can remember it quite clearly. As I mentioned earlier, we lived just around the corner from St. Stephen's Green.

On that Easter Monday, my parents had gone off to play golf at Malahide which is about eleven miles north of Dublin. In the morning, my nurse brought me for a walk along one side of Stephen's Green. Near the then Vincent's Hospital we saw a group of men standing out on the road carrying picks and shovels. We wondered what they were doing there on a holiday with only a few other people around. Later on we learned that they were the rebel advance party, about to dig themselves into the Green, and that they

The Shelbourne Hotel, which was taken over by the British during the rebellion. It gave them the perfect stronghold from which to control St. Stephen's Green. (Photograph taken in 1912).

would be holding those trenches with guns later in the day!

When we returned home, we heard that the rebellion had broken out. We also heard that all the railway bridges had been blown up, and as a result that my parents were almost certainly stranded in Malahide. I remember very clearly kneeling on the window-seat in the study, looking out at the street below and feeling a terrible anxiety building up. The day passed very slowly. It was late supper-time before my parents managed to get home and to tell us their story.

A friend with a car had given them a lift from Malahide to the bottom of Grafton Street. From there they had walked up to the top end where it meets Stephen's Green. There a taxi passed them carrying a British officer. It came up Grafton Street and headed straight on towards the College of Surgeons, and as it passed along the side of the Green the guns opened up from within the railings. The officer lay down flat on the floor of the taxi as it sped on. However, when it came to the Harcourt Street corner they found that there was a road-block there and they had to turn around and come back, "running the gauntlet" all over again. My parents, still rooted to the spot in astonishment, now realised that they would soon be in the line of fire. They ran left towards the Stephen's Green Club where my father was a member. There they knocked and knocked until they were let in by the frightened staff, and were passed out through the mews at the back. They found their way safely home by various back lanes.

Summerhill, looking west towards Gardiner Street (1916). Just moments after taking this photograph, Aunt Maud came under fire from the British soldiers located at the barricade (which is just visible on the street below).

My father was very concerned about the safety of his mother and his sister, Maud, who still lived right in the middle of Dublin, not far from the GPO itself. By all accounts it was the principal building under fire. Their house was next to the factory in Summerhill where my family had been making carriages for one hundred and fifty years or so. I was always a bit intimidated by my Aunt Maud. She wore somewhat masculine-type clothes, and like the Boy-Scouts she was "always prepared". She carried one of everything she might need - such as a knife, scissors, string, needles, safety-pins, a bandage etc. She often had to search for things in various mysterious pockets hidden beneath her skirts. However, on this occasion it was her new panoramic camera which would be getting her into trouble!

While Sackville Street (now O'Connell Street) and the GPO were being pounded into rubble by the British guns, she went up on the roof every day to see what was happening. She hoped to get a good and perhaps telling photograph. But as she was wearing a dark felt hat, she was taken to be a rebel sniper and the British soldiers started shooting at HER! She had to take cover very fast!!

The rebels held out for one week before surrendering. Aunt Maud ventured out soon afterwards, and she managed to take some wonderful photographs of the GPO and the surrounding streets, some of which are reproduced here.

Eden Quay, just to the east of Hopkins and Hopkins (1916).

Two views of O'Connell Street (1916). The first shows the corner with Lower Abbey Street, the second looks south towards the O'Connell Monument. Aunt Maud took these with a panoramic camera, which adds an interesting perspective to some familiar scenes.

The Metropole Hotel and, next door, the General Post Office (1916). The GPO was reduced to just the outside walls and took some time to rebuild. It would come into my life much later on, when I worked for RTE in their radio studios on the top floor.

Two more views of O'Connell Street (1916).
The first looks north in the direction of Sackville Place, and the second shows the forlorn shell that was Clerys and the Imperial Hotel.

Liberty Hall and Brooks Thomas (1916). This is the usual route we would have taken to get to the city centre. My father worked in Brooks Thomas for many years. When the rebellion broke out, he was concerned about the safety of the two hundred horses which were stabled behind the Brooks Thomas' offices. My father was able to contact the man who was supposed to be looking after them, and was very relieved later on to find out that he had been able to get to them safely by crawling on hands and knees along the lane leading to the stables. He then fed and watered them, which action was much appreciated by the management (and by the horses too, no doubt).

We are not certain about the location of these photographs, although we believe that the first is in Lower Abbey Street and the second is in Eden Quay (1916). It's extraordinary how much damage the British created in their attempts to overcome the rebels. After all, they could have just waited for a few weeks and starved them out.

My mother (second left) inspects the damage in O'Connell Street (1916).

Another view of Clerys, this time showing the massive internal damage caused by the British shelling (1916).

Henry Street, looking east towards Nelson's Pillar (1916). The Coliseum Theatre remains standing on the right. This photograph must have been taken only a day or two after the end of the fighting - the crowds are still being held back, but most of the rubble remains uncleared.

We had snipers on our own roofs in Upper Pembroke Street, and all around Fitzwilliam Square. Luckily, my father had had the foresight to break out a door from our back yard into a laneway running alongside our house. We were able to come and go that way in order to lay in supplies from the local shop in Baggot Street. This was providential at the time, although we came to regret it later on when we had moved out of Upper Pembroke Street to a new house in the suburbs.

In the intervening years, our old house had been converted into flats for use by British officers. Sadly, it was one of the locations in which the "Bloody Sunday" murders took place on Sunday morning, November 21, 1920. The officers were shot cold-bloodedly in their beds, on the orders of Michael Collins. Of course, he was only responding to some earlier British atrocities but that didn't make us feel any better at the time.

My father was devastated! He felt that if he hadn't made that door the rebels would neither have got in to start with nor have been able to escape afterwards. It was indeed horrible to think that this had happened in the old home in which I had been born, and of which I had such happy memories.

Grannie Hutton, Aunt Maud (right) and me (1921).

Minnie And Maud And Me

Minnie was a fairy - I mean IS a fairy. I know because she's always there ... I mean here ... Oh! I am confused.

Minnie works mostly in secret. When I asked her why, she said 'It's not in secret. I'm in sight for all who can see, and if you can't see it's because you don't have absolute faith.' Minnie is a very positive fairy and always knows the answer.

'No-one,' she went on, 'can see us fairies unless they believe in us.' I think this is true, because I don't ever remember seeing Minnie, but she seems to have no trouble communicating with me and is always present when I need her.

'And,' she continued, 'even if you could see me, I might not be what you had expected. Do you remember Minnie the black hen?'

'Of course I do - was that you?'

Minnie positively cackled with delight. I remembered visiting my Grandmother and my Aunt Maud at their house on Summerhill in Dublin, beside the carriage factory. I learned that Minnie was the name of my aunt's favourite black Minorca hen, which used to perch upon her shoulder.

'I loved to lay free range eggs for your dear Grandmother,' went on Minnie.

'Free range! How did you manage that when you were kept on the top floor of the house in Summerhill?'

'We-e-ll,' crooned Minnie. 'Maybe there was a small bit of magic present -' and she broke into her "Successful Laying Song" ... Pk Pk Pk Pk ...

I wasn't surprised, as I had always believed that the coach-building factory next door was full of magic. So many beautiful carriages had been produced there. Once I asked my father if they had made Cinderella's coach for her to go to the ball, and he had looked so serious as he replied 'Maybe, maybe they did. They certainly could have but maybe they would have had difficulty in finding an Irish Pumpkin!' But I firmly believed that they would have been successful.

Family outing over the Featherbed Road, Glencree (1913).

Of course at that stage carriages were a thing of the past and motor cars were "in". John Hutton and Sons brought some of the first motor cars into Ireland, and my Aunt Maud must have been one of the first women drivers. She drove Grannie on many an outing, even as far as Luggala in County Wicklow. In those early years the passengers had to be prepared to get out when climbing a steep hill. I clearly remember running behind the car, carrying blocks of wood to put behind the wheels when the driver stopped to let the boiling engine cool down!

I often felt very much in awe of Aunt Maud and found her somewhat intimidating. She had no gift for managing children but got on very well with her hens who were treated as pets and were all given individual names. As she and Grannie had no garden she kept them on deep litter in the inter-connecting attic rooms of the two tall, thin houses next door to the factory. They even took the hens with them each summer, when they rented a house in the country!

On one occasion I went to stay with them in their rented house - I think it was located in Delgany. They had a domestic called Ella, who liked children and who did her best to look after me. (I gather that I was a bit of a "handful" at that age.) One lovely summer day Ella was out beating a carpet in the garden, when I took the beater from her and started beating her! I can't remember why, except that I thought her "very dim" and of course I considered that she was only "a servant". This attitude was all part of my background. My parents were very kind to their domestics but they were always regarded as servants - almost a lesser species. "Upstairs/Downstairs" was taken for granted by everybody. Ella was a great big "softie" who was almost twice my height, but she did nothing but turn her back and cover her head and moan 'Oh, Miss Louise! Oh, Miss Louise!' whilst I walloped away gleefully as hard as I could.

Suddenly a voice roared 'LOUISE!' from behind me and my heart nearly stopped as I realised Aunt Maud had caught me red-handed! I can't remember my punishment - all I can remember was the shock and the humiliation as I was "cut down to size" in front of Ella, and the knowledge that I hated my aunt!

Grannie Hutton and her much-loved hens (1921).

'Yes,' said Minnie, 'but your Aunt was so very kind under her rather brusque manner. She was that rather rare person who always spoke her mind with perfect integrity. Do you remember how beautifully she played the piano?'

And suddenly I remembered how, when Aunt Maud came to dinner, I would be wrapped up in a blanket and allowed to sit on the stairs and listen to her playing Chopin Nocturnes and Preludes, especially the one with the "galloping horses" in the left hand.

After this there is a great big gap in my memories of Aunt Maud, but you will be glad to hear that later on in life we became good friends. When Grannie died, Aunt Maud took off around the world staying as often as not with friends, one of whom lived in Tanganyka, East Africa. She loved Africa so much that she bought a farm of her own and ran it with the help of a native work force. Once again she demonstrated her knack of being prepared for anything, even to the extent of taking a course on car maintenance before she went out there, and bringing a truckful of spare parts in case of breakdown in the wild.

She stayed out there, all on her own, until her health broke down and she came home. I came to know her quite well then and found that we had a lot in common. She was so different - even loveable. Maybe she had found out that however self-reliant one makes oneself, we all need other people in the end.

'Or perhaps it was you that had grown up,' said Minnie. 'You could appreciate what a remarkable woman she was!' and Minnie faded out as she often did when she had made her point.

We certainly shared a rich family heritage - Minnie and Maud and me.

Switzerland

Whenever there is a fall of snow in this country, which really covers the landscape, I get "Swiss-sick!" Especially so if there is no wind to disperse the soft white covering on each tiny twig, each leaf, each gatepost and each wire and all "a-sparkle" in the warming sunshine. Tap a branch and a scintillating cloud of fresh powder snow fills the air. Walk on the crunchy white blanket covering the fields and your footprints remain until the thaw with those of the animals or the birds who were there before you. I can distinguish between those of fox or badger or rabbit - very distinctive the rabbit - and here, what are these, with the long spaces between ... Oh! of course, it's my own dog leaping along so joyfully in front of me in the clean crisp air.

In 1921, when I was about ten years old my parents went off on their own for a short holiday in Switzerland. Two weeks later they came home vowing they would never go again without taking us - my two brothers and me - as they thought it was a veritable paradise for children. So we all went winter-sporting the following Christmas holidays, and enjoyed it so much that we continued to do so for the next ten years or so.

It was quite a journey in those days - exciting enough on its own. First we had the Irish sea to cross which could be so rough. The crossing took all of four and a half hours in those days, after which we had to endure another seven or eight hours on a long train journey across north Wales and the English midlands. It necessitated staying a night in London on the way. We usually fitted in a theatre either going or coming. Then came the Channel crossing which often caused great queasiness for both my Mum and me. (She was a very poor sailor. Just going aboard was enough to make her feel sick.) This was followed by the anxiety of finding the right French sleeper train in the dark and hoping that the travel agent had got it right with regard to the numbers of our compartments. In fact, Thomas Cook often got it wrong, or perhaps it was the sleeping-car attendant who served early comers first, but there always seemed to be much anxious searching before it was sorted out.

The French trains looked huge and threatening because there were no built up platforms, only steep steps up to each carriage. We had to struggle with our hand-luggage, whilst trying to catch up with the porter already half-way along to the other end. I was always afraid that the train, which kept on puffing out steam at intervals as if about to depart, would move on before we caught up with him, or that he would depart to look for a second fare and leave our luggage behind on the platform. Thankfully we always did get settled in eventually. We didn't have any difficulty in getting to sleep after the attendant brought us a good hot cup of tea - which my father (who never travelled without his flask of whiskey) laced with a drop of "the crather"!

In fact I enjoyed the fierce rhythm of these fast trains - clackety-clack, clackety-clack - rocketing along in the dark through the low countries. From time to time, we would be interrupted by customs officials who switched on lights but seldom bothered to wake us up, so exhausted were we. When I shut my eyes, I could picture myself being cradled and rocked by this rushing monster, and I was soon fast asleep again. We would reach Switzerland in the early hours, but were usually allowed to sleep on until it was time to change trains. Then we looked forward to a continental breakfast aboard a Swiss mountain train. This usually consisted of delicious, freshly baked croissants and apricot jam. These were, by contrast, gentle little trains from which we could watch the entrancing Swiss countryside unfold before our eyes.

We climbed steadily up the valleys, and saw the great mountain peaks gradually coming into view. Sometimes, to my delight, at the end of the train journey, we would be packed into a horse-drawn sleigh with chiming bells on the harness, and with a great sheepskin covering pulled right up to our chins. Then we would be driven to our hotel, with our luggage following safely behind in another sleigh. The Swiss were adept at giving everybody a warm welcome and perfect service.

Next day we would visit the ski shop as soon as possible, to hire and fit our skis, ski-sticks and ski-boots - the latter very carefully fitted. If they were too big there would be no proper control of the skis and a possible broken ankle. If they were too small, there would be no room for thick socks - so cold feet! We usually hired our skates and boots also - all the heavy items - but would bring our own ski-suits. This achieved, we would hurry to try them all out on the nearby practice slopes, where there would be nothing very steep or difficult.

My friend, Biddy Darley (right) and me (1928).

The ski slopes in those days were very easy as we had to do our own climbing with the help of "skins". These really were actual skins of animals with long hairs which pointed one way only. They would be attached to the sliding surface of our skis so that we could slide forward whilst they prevented us from sliding backwards. There were no ski-lifts in those early days, and cable cars had yet to be invented. There was a funicular, or mountain railway, in most resorts, as at Zermatt, one of our favourite places. The railway could take us up from the village at 4,000 feet to the Gornergrat at 7,000 feet. But to get to the end of the railway line at 10,000 feet we had to climb the last leg on our own. This was very hard work at that altitude, and I used to get very breathless near the top. I was glad to get a gentle push in the back from our guide. But oh! - the views which opened up were spectacular.

Our special favourite was the Matterhorn, that wonderfully shaped peak which has lured so many people, near to the border between German-speaking Switzerland and Italy. We would follow the line of the railway as we climbed, with rising ground on our right but with the beautiful untouched ski-slopes on our left. We would soon be descending these after having had some hot soup and sandwiches in the little terminus restaurant at the top. We always had a guide with us after fresh snow, as there would be no tracks to follow and we could easily stray into avalanche country, or lose ourselves in the woods above Zermatt.

My brothers, who were a good deal older than me, liked to get out on the upper unspoilt slopes as soon as possible. They felt that their holidays were so short they didn't want to lose time on the practice slopes learning the safe way to do things! In fact, they always went straight down every slope regardless! As they were both fine athletes with good balance they usually survived, but there were times when they paid the price.

Oh! it is wonderful to be out in this clean, fresh air! (1928)

My elder brother, Wilfred, already more than 20 years old, put his shoulder out on two separate occasions and spoiled two of his holidays. My second brother, Walter, tended to break his ski-points and had to carry a spare pair in his knapsack. The first time this happened was on one of our Gornergrat trips, and we had no spare points with us. With no upturned point the ski tends to dig into the snow instead of sliding over it, and really means ski-ing on the one good leg only - a very difficult balancing act. It meant fall after fall for poor Walter, and very slow progress for all three of us. It was dark before we got down to the paths above Zermatt where he could take off his skis and walk the rest of the way. Meanwhile our parents were distraught with worry about us, and were just about to send out a search party!

My parents didn't ski. They tried it once and felt they were too old. However, they both skated well and enjoyed the sunny, sheltered skating rink belonging to the hotel. We sometimes joined them there, especially on gymkhana days which were great fun. My father liked to join the curling club, and my mother - being Scottish - supported him there. They also hired "luges", little toboggans which they could pull along. They would walk through the village with them until they found a suitable slope on the road where they could use them. I sometimes accompanied them on my skis.

Family and friends gather on the ice (1922). I am on the extreme right, beside my first-ever "sweetheart"!

I loved to explore these attractive villages, and would follow the little paths leading round to the backs of the beautifully carved chalets. On one occasion, I found a little unspoilt slope of snow and thought I would try some of my turns. Unfortunately, I had an unexpected fall into a small hidden stream and couldn't get out! The trouble was that the snow had bridged the narrow ditch and I never saw it until I had gone head first into it and my skis had stuck across the top. There I was suspended upside down with my head just above running water! I shouted for help but nobody heard, and I began to get desperate. I kicked and wriggled so hard that I managed to turn one ski around, and down, and then could free the other. I finally emerged wet and shaken, and vowed never to ski alone again - even on the flat!

Swiss sunsets were astonishing and beautiful. The sinking sun turned the snowy peaks to a gorgeous ice-cream pink, which turned to deepest rose which - suddenly - was gone. Darkness came down with little warning. After dark was *après ski* time and everyone did their own thing. Walter, who had a very sweet tooth, looked forward to an extravagant Swiss *patisserie* with a cup of chocolate - an expensive extra. Wilfred might go to an *après ski* dance for which he didn't have to change from ski clothes. I didn't care for dancing in heavy ski-boots and preferred to tuck up under my cosy duvet, and to have a snooze before changing for dinner about 7 p.m.

After dinner, we would have plenty of dancing in the hotel ballroom. Wilfred and I loved dancing, but Walter hadn't yet got over his extreme shyness. One night there was a special dance which allowed the girls to ask the boys for a change. There was a long pause to start with, and then a young girl came very nervously right across the floor and asked Walter to dance - and he refused! She had to retreat, blushing madly, across the still empty floor. We entreated him to go and ask her for the next dance, but he wouldn't, and he in his turn blushed furiously and retreated to his bed! But by the next summer holidays he had learnt the "Charleston" and we couldn't stop him dancing it all round the house! He never waited any more for the girls to ask him first!

Every now and then they would announce an Ice Carnival by night, and the skating rink would be lit with fairy lights. We would be asked to carry most intriguing lanterns on sticks while dancing to the hotel musicians. Never a great skater, I liked to draw aside occasionally to where I could watch the gay scene, and also see the mountains lit by the moon and many stars. Serene, with a cold purity, they made a perfect setting for the sparkling jewel-like skating rink below. Switzerland was nearly as wonderful by night as it was by day, for both young and old.

Christmas Card

I have a Christmas card sitting in front of me on the kitchen table. To one side of me is a work-top - untidy as usual - where the telephone lives. At the right-hand end of this there is a letter-rack full of old stationery, with cards, and such like, that are seldom disturbed. Five minutes ago I was trying to squeeze a packet of new envelopes into the rack when this Christmas card fell out at my feet. I was amazed at the coincidence, partly because it had probably been in the rack for some thirty or forty years, and partly because the writer, Sally Wilson, used to bring me to school. I had just been trying to remember details of this period in order to write it up! With Sally's card in my hand the memories came flooding back. It was indeed a strange coincidence - or "synchronicity" as Jung would term it.

The Wilsons were great friends of ours who lived at the other side of Fitzwilliam Square. Each morning, I would be brought as far as their house in time to walk to school with Sally who was several years older than me. There were no school buses or cars to take us in those days. The Wilson's house was only a short walk from the Grand Canal, which had to be crossed on the way to school. Unfortunately, I was very scared of this canal, as Mrs. Wilson - Sally's mother, whom I never liked - had told me there was "a bad man" hiding behind each of the big old trees lining the banks. She said that he would jump out at us if we went too near! So I would hold on very tightly to Sally's hand until we were well over Leeson Street Bridge, on our way to Miss Wilson's School (no relation) at the top end of Ailesbury Road. There we would part company as I was in the kindergarten and Sally was a senior girl in her final year.

Sally's father was Judge Wilson, who, I think, must have come from Northern Ireland originally. Later on, during the "troubles", he became involved in various IRA trials, as a result of which he received several death threats. He didn't hang about to discover if the threats were real, but moved immediately up to Belfast with his whole family. I lost contact with Sally for quite a long time, although our families kept in touch during our summer holidays when we all met in Newcastle, County Down. By then, I had found a friend of my own age, Jean Rotherham, and we were allowed complete freedom as long as we stayed together. I remember my joy in going barefoot and wearing any old clothes - we even liked to wear my brothers' shorts on occasion. This must have been before Ireland was partitioned in 1921, and the iniquitous border was set up.

Family trip to Newcastle (1919). Jean (third right) was my first "true friend".

At that age I was impervious to politics. My clearest memory is of going with my brother, Walter, and his pal Ted Rotherham - Jean's brother - to stay on their farm in County Leitrim. This was my first introduction to farm life. Our biggest thrill was that Ted had been given an airgun for his birthday. We used to spend a lot of our time in their great big farm-yard, shooting at the rats which were to be seen on a big pile of sacks of feeding stuff in the centre. All four of us would lie on our tummies in the doorway of one of the sheds, with the gun ready trained on the sacks until the rats appeared, and then try to hit them. The rats disappeared for a short while after every shot, but they always reappeared and we waited patiently in the warm sunshine. We all took turns and Ted was very fair in letting us girls have a go. Actually, I don't think we ever managed to hit anything. Certainly, I don't remember any dead bodies, but that might be my selective memory working overtime again. I never noticed any other farming events, such as cows and harvesting and the like! I had no idea then that I would end up farming myself in my middle age, but more about that later.

Sally only reappears much later on in my story. In the meanwhile I had been to two boarding schools. The first was Hillcourt in Glenageary, up above Dún Laoghaire. The thing I remember most about being there was going swimming down at the sea, and how tired I used to feel as we climbed up the long hill afterwards, in a long crocodile line. I used to admire one or two of the braver girls who slipped out of the line, without being seen by the equally tired teacher in charge, so that they could buy sweets! In 1927, when I was 15, two of my friends transferred to an English school in Berkshire called Downe House. I asked my parents if I could go with them, and they agreed. We travelled together and my next really vivid memory is of the last part of our long journey. We were in the train travelling down from London to Reading and we realised suddenly that we would soon be there. Extreme fear hit me then and I felt like crawling under the seats and hiding!

The "Three Irishes" - my good self, Biddy Darley and Nan Franks (1927).

Needless to say, it wasn't as bad as we feared. As we always clung together we were known as the "Three Irishes"! Soon I was wishing that we could have got there much earlier. The two schools were so different. In Hillcourt, the key thing was to avoid work and to learn as little as possible! At Downe House, the attitude was quite different and people wanted to achieve something. Many students took additional classes after school hours. For example, we had a wonderful oboe player who was already playing in an adult orchestra even though she was only in her teens. She did more music than anything else. I would probably have got into acting there, as they had an exciting outdoor Greek theatre in which they put on a Shakespeare play every summer. I might even have gone on to a school of acting much earlier than I actually did, and as a result could have changed the course of my life.

As it was, I didn't stay on with the other two for long as I was sent off to learn French with a family in Paris.

Paris

My French family consisted of Monsieur and Madame Dèsaubliaux and their two boys, Raoul and Henri. They lived in the Auteuil district of Paris. The boys were only thirteen and fourteen years old and so were not much help to me, as a young shy girl of nineteen. In fact, I didn't see much of them as they were at school all day, then spent the evening eating and sharing a bath and so to bed in preparation for the next day's early start. I found it frustrating, as I could hear them chattering away to each another in the hot steamy bathroom - next door to my own room but a world away nonetheless. I think also that I was still a bit of a "snob".

Back home, my two brothers had been sent off to a public boarding school to gain their "old school tie" friends, and the girls like me were sent abroad to gain some "polish"! But in France, the boys were all sent to the same day schools as everybody else and didn't bring homework back with them, as they did it in school, together with various games. They only got home in time for the evening meal, but with no books to carry to and fro. Before I left France, I realised that I preferred the French way of doing things.

I proved this to my own satisfaction when I came back to pay a short visit to the Dèsaubliaux family four or five years later on, by which time Raoul and Henri had matured and had become two most charming young men. They went out of their way to entertain me by taking me everywhere with them, introducing me to their friends and to their sports clubs. I wished they had been that age when I arrived originally all shy and "gawky" straight from school.

I was only meant to stay in Paris for six months, but by that time I could hardly speak a word of French and wrote home in despair to ask my parents if I could stay on for another six months. If this was too difficult money-wise, I suggested that they should 'Please sell my grandmother's diamond which she left me in her will, to pay for it!' Well, I was granted my wish and given another six months, but they never sold my diamond which I still wear on special occasions. I must admit that I would have been surprised if they had, knowing my generous parents!

Anyway, I made good use of my extra time. I joined a *Cours d'Étranger* at the Sorbonne which I attended every day. I took down copious notes written in French and, as I was able to listen without interruption, I slowly began to make sense of what the Dèsaubliaux family were saying - they all talked at the same time - and to speak a little myself. Now I was able to enjoy Parisian culture to the full. I went to the Opera every week and did all the sights with the "Blue Book" (guide to Paris) in my hand. As to clothes, I was wearing little better than my school things and my comfortable flat-heeled brogue shoes. Mme. Dèsaubliaux used to laugh at me in what she called *Mes Bateaux*, and would try to encourage me to look after my appearance - but all to no avail at this stage of my development.

I loved Paris. It seemed to have a special character of its own starting with wonderful Notre Dame, centred on the Ile de la Cité in the midst of the River Seine. I felt that it was packed full of French history. Although it should have been easily defended, it suffered several invasions which necessitated rebuilding it time and time again. This meant that the same style of architecture tended to predominate, and Notre Dame seemed all of a piece, even though its two square towers didn't quite match and the soaring Arc Boutants were a late addition. Not far away is the Sainte Chapelle, a veritable "architects dream". When one stood within it, it felt as if one were actually part of a beautiful, stained glass window - a memorable experience. The next excitement was to go up the Champs-Elysées to the Arc de Triomphe and the Unknown Soldier's Tomb. Not to forget the Eiffel Tower and the unbelievable restaurant perched at the top, with views of all Paris spread out far below.

There was one special week when all the architectural gems were spotlighted after dark, and Monsieur Dèsaubliaux took us in his car to see them. Of course, we visited the Louvre with its famous pictures, although I have to admit that I never really appreciated the Mona Lisa! When my parents came to visit, I shocked Madame Dèsaubliaux by buying expensive tickets for them to go to *Les Folies Bergères*, with the many naked ladies they would see there. But after all, as they didn't speak French, then where else could they go? It was expected of "sexy" Paris anyway! These shows were so marvellously well done, with wonderful artistes, such as Maurice Chevalier and Mistinguette. We actually heard Chevalier himself singing *Every Little Breeze Seems To Whisper Louise*, with straw hat and all. It was something very special. My parents loved the whole show, and afterwards I was able to take them up to Montmartre and the church of the Sacré Coeur, and to sample lovely hot pancakes cooked in the open while enjoying the view of the Paris lights spread out below. It was such a happy occasion and I'm glad I have it all to remember.

I could now be considered as "finished". That is to say my education was completed, but I didn't feel "finished" since I didn't have a single idea in my mind as to what came next! True, I could now make myself understood in French and had absorbed a smattering of French culture, but to what end? I had heard enough operas to do me for a lifetime, but I much preferred the straight plays I was just only beginning to be able to understand. However, I kept busy finishing my Christmas shopping before leaving wonderful, but expensive, Paris.

I hoped to be inspired come the New Year.

Spring Dialogue

You say it's Spring, but how do you know
On this dark grey steamy day?
The swelling buds are showing green
So Spring is on its way.

Wind is howling, blowing roofs off
Ground is hard with frost.
Snowdrops flowering, daffs in bud
A Bumble Bee seems lost.

Stormy winds bring heavy showers
Who would be our guests?
Swallows winging, all birds singing,
Madly building nests.

Days of heavy chilling rain -
Will early lambs survive?
When mothers share their body-heat
And warming milk - they thrive!

Puppies, kittens, fluffy chickens,
Young of every kind
Tell you that it's Spring right now -
Refresh your aged mind.

Medical Gymnastics

I returned home to Dublin, supposedly able to take my place in the world. The trouble was that I was no nearer knowing what to do with my life. It never seems to have occurred to me to do nothing. I always took it for granted that I would have a job, or preferably a profession, and this is where Sally Wilson comes into the story again. In 1931, she came to visit my mother, in our new house outside Donnybrook to which we had moved some time earlier. Sally informed us she was now a fully trained physio-therapist. She said that she was working very hard and thoroughly enjoying it, and she gave us such a full description that it took my fancy and I decided to do the same.

I trained at the Hume Street School of Massage in Dublin, under Miss Allen and Miss Hetty Micks. I ended up with a whole lot of letters after my name which sounded very impressive - CSMMG (Chartered Society of Massage and Medical Gymnastics), ME (Medical Electricity) and, last but not least, LET (Light and Electro-Therapy). Nowadays, it's all lumped together under the title of Physio-therapy. I must confess that I never really discovered what was meant by "Medical Gymnastics" - was it I who performed the gymnastics in doing my job, or was it my patient as the result of my expert work? I still don't know! It was a three year course which included six months practical experience working in a hospital.

I remember travelling every morning by tram from Donnybrook to Stephen's Green, then walking down York Street - which was an abominable slum at that time - to the Adelaide Hospital where we massaged all sorts and shapes of bodies. It was a very big department, but we were constantly under the eagle eye of an experienced physio. Although the training was good as far as it went, and very interesting (I took a special interest in learning about "muscle actions" and the complex balance maintained between the different muscle groups), I never felt that it equipped us sufficiently to decide what the treatment should be of the various cases sent to us by the doctors. They often didn't give us any help. For instance, a note accompanying a patient could read just "sprained ankle" and the physio would have to decide what the damage was, and how to treat it. Sometimes there wasn't even an X-ray to help pinpoint the problem.

So when I was asked to do a "locum" down in Tipperary, treating a teenager who had a bad leg after falling off her horse during a hunt, I felt like refusing to go. However, there was no-one else available and my friends told me how lucky I was to be offered a job so soon after finishing. I might not be offered another if I turned this one down. When I considered that I would be earning my first salary ever, I decided to give it a try.

I travelled down-country by train and arrived at Thurles in the early evening. I was met by a large car and driven to an imposing country house surrounded by fields. It took at least five domestics to run it: cook, scullery maid, parlour maid, house maid and finally the "tweeny" whose job it was to keep the open fires going. They were supposed to keep this frigid house from freezing solid. I never felt so cold! There was no central heating and no visible electricity. My hostess said it was bad for the eyes and she preferred oil lamps or candles. Privately, I thought she felt her wrinkles would show less by candlelight as she was well into her forties. I had never been to bed by candlelight before and found it quite an experience. The first night I was guided by the "tweeny" who lit two candles for me in the huge, featureless guestroom. However, the following night I had to find my own shaky way up the dark, creaky old house. My candle did quite a lot of shaking as well!

My patient had what they called a "concertina" leg. Her brother, who considered himself a bit of a wit, said I could either "cure it or play it". Actually, this really described the situation better than he realised! She was about sixteen, and when she tried to walk, the big muscle - quadriceps - on the front of her thigh would go into spasm in ridges across it. I had never seen anything like it and didn't have a clue what to do next. I didn't say so to my hosts as I had been taught that I must retain my patient's confidence. But when they asked how long it would take to get better, I was honest enough to say I didn't know. All I could do was to teach her to relax with a cushion under her knee, and to keep her weight off it for the time being. I gradually added some simple exercises to keep the other muscles going, and some gentle massage. To my everlasting relief it worked and she began to get better. But I really think that she would have recovered whether or not I was there!

They put up with me for a fortnight, feeding me (still by candlelight) and providing books and a healthy walk up the fields each day. But they questioned me more and more often about how long it would take to cure it. The doctor wanted me to stay, but it became obvious to me that he didn't know any more than I did. Perhaps he believed that at least I brought a bit of common sense into that "huntin'" household, but I felt they were becoming more and more sceptical. Finally, the pressure became too much and I told them I could do no more for her. Then relief flooded over all of us, while I packed my bag and departed for home again.

Other cases came my way including another problem patient. It was a small boy about seven years old who had damaged a wrist but wouldn't allow anyone to touch it. Having been forewarned, I just turned up and brought a book to read to him. I had a small suitcase with me and he asked what was in it. I told him it contained my overalls and some massage powder, but he was very suspicious. I told him to open it to see for himself and only then did he begin to trust me. I imagine that he remembered having injections which hurt and now was determined to avoid a repetition. I asked him to open the suitcase himself each time to see what I had brought him - a ball or a game or something he could do with his wrist. Soon he was looking forward to his treatments, and I began to think I would like to specialise in treating children.

This notion was reinforced in my mind by my experience with a very overweight patient who needed to slim. In those days, we still believed that weight loss could be achieved by massage and passive exercises. So I gave her one hour of '"general treatment" every day for a month. Of course, it was I who lost the weight and my patient - if anything - put it on! It made up my mind for me, and I announced that I would treat only children in future.

I also decided to do a course in radiography which I found fascinating. It would take a year to do in London as at that time there were no Irish courses available. I had the idea that I would be able to combine physiotherapy and radiography for children. As it turned out, I settled for becoming a radiographer in the Children's Hospital in Harcourt Street. I had intended to to add the physiotherapy later on, but I never did as I found the radiography very demanding. I had a wonderful radiologist named Dr. McDonogh who approved fully of my efforts to make the X-ray department less frightening for

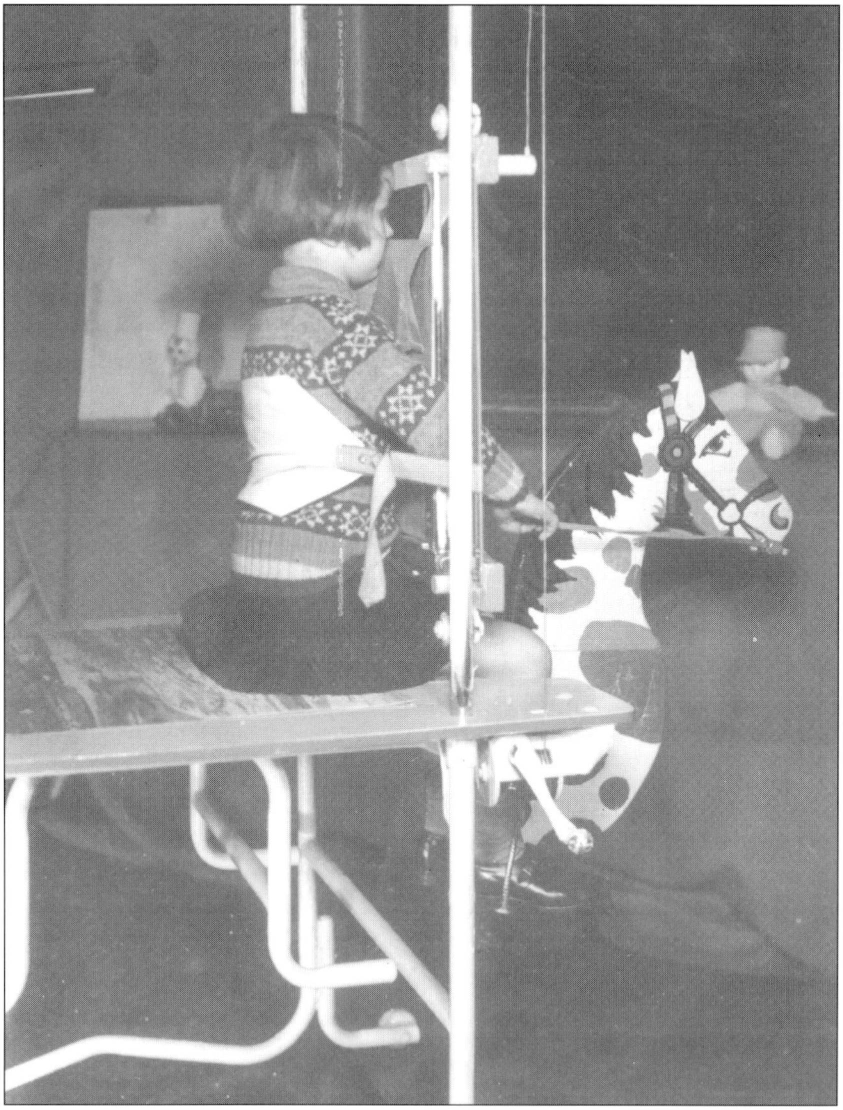

The X-Ray Horse at the Children's Hospital in Harcourt Street, Dublin (1936).

the children. I invented a special chest X-ray stand with a horse's head attached. There was a bridle to hold and stirrups to put their feet in and the children loved it. They would sit calmly and without fear on the "X-ray horse" and we got better X-rays as a result. We sent a photograph in to the Chartered Society of Radiographers and a special prize was awarded to the hospital.

We also wore soft blue overalls instead of alarming white, and I supplied some toys for the children to play with while they waited. Dr. McDonogh came twice a week to read the X-rays and I would make a pot of tea. Soon the senior staff would join us and discuss their patients' results with Dr. McDonogh over a "cuppa". We became quite popular. So in 1936, when I received the very surprising and quite unexpected invitation to go to America with the Irish women's hockey team, not only did Dr. McDonogh give me his blessing, but the Hospital Board gave me six weeks leave to make the trip of a lifetime!

The Irish Hockey team which toured Philadelphia in 1936. As far as I can remember, they are: Vera Mahoney, Kathleen Kirkwood, Deirdre Ennis, Doris Findlater, Louise Hutton, Janet Croome, Gretta Mahoney, Patricia Thompson, Cherry Symes, Clare Parsons and Binkie Harman.

America

America! How on earth did I get there? Answer - sheer luck!

I was asked to join the Irish hockey team which took part in an international hockey tournament in Philadelphia in October 1936, and which toured Pennsylvania immediately afterwards. I had played hockey at school, and afterwards for a team called the "Maids of the Mountain" (our hockey field was in view of Three Rock Mountain). I did take part in the Leinster Trials, but I never reached the Irish team when it played at home. The selectors had to go a long way down the list to reach me - that's where the luck came in. Perhaps it was at a time of year when people couldn't leave their jobs, or had exams, or were just short of cash. I was in the "good books" of the Children's Hospital at the time, and as I have explained they very kindly gave me time off to do the trip. My supportive parents bought my ticket for me.

Our tour started from Belfast where we boarded the *SS Transylvania*, which belonged to the Anchor Line, a small Scottish shipping company. At that time, it took all of eight days to reach New York. It was my first long sea trip, but after a day or two I found my sea-legs and enjoyed every minute of it.

We had four days in New York which made a wonderful start. We stayed in the Taft Hotel on the 17th floor, which felt quite high to us, and followed this with breakfast in the Rainbow Room of Radio City on the 67th floor. Next we were taken up the Empire State Building to the 104th floor, from where we were fortunate enough to see the evening sunset. The glow from the sun lit up one side of each of the many skyscrapers and turned them to a warm apricot colour. This contrasted with the deep blue of the water surrounding

New York on three sides. It was a truly stupendous view which was worth coming all the way to America to see on its own - quite unforgettable.

I wouldn't like to live in New York, however. At ground level one feels so shut in at the bottom of a dark chasm full of bustling people and noise. Oh! the constant noise. There was no greenery apart from Central Park. That was large and beautiful, but you would have had to be rich to live in sight of it. There were many exquisite shops, but they were so expensive. As you might expect, we were not taken to see the poorer parts of the city.

The next day we went sight-seeing by boat. First we took a closer look at the great Statue of Liberty which had welcomed so many oppressed people from across the wide Atlantic, especially the Irish in famine times. Then we went to Ellis Island where the survivors were landed from the over-crowded sailing ships, often known as "coffin ships", which had taken them aboard, perhaps in faraway Cork.

Ellis Island was unimpressive with regard to its buildings, but it was heavy with atmosphere. I could imagine the anxiety which these exhausted people must have been feeling. They could actually see New York across the harbour, but they would have been wondering whether or not they would be accepted and allowed into America, and then would they find work. What would happen if they didn't? Many of them had risked everything to buy their ticket, and would have had no reserves. Hopes would have risen as they were cleaned up, deloused and fed properly. Many had relatives or friends who had made the courageous journey before them. Their predecessors would have sent home money, together with descriptions of this fabulous country and its opportunities. Their eyes would have been constantly drawn across the water to the curved wall of great skyscrapers, with the big ships moored fanwise right up to their feet.

I wasn't sorry when the time came to move on to Philadelphia. There were no great sky-scrapers to visit, but we got a great welcome from our hostesses who swept us off in small batches to their own homes. We gathered that ours was a very wealthy family, but we never had the courage to ask if we were staying with a millionaire! Nancy, the daughter, led us to her big car, and another car always followed close behind. She explained that she was never allowed to go out in one car without backup, just in case she was kidnapped. We felt very sorry for her. When we got to her home, we entered through a spacious hall with many display cabinets filled with valuable artifacts - beautiful to look at, but depressingly like a museum.

We liked Nancy and her family very much when we got to know them. They were very good to us. But I wouldn't swap lives with them for any fortune! They told us they were building a new house in the country and one day after our match we were taken to see it. We were driving across rather flat, uninteresting country when Nancy said 'There it is.' We saw a large, impressive mansion with about thirty to forty cars parked in front of it.

'Oh!' we said. 'We didn't know there was a party here,' and looked down wistfully at our dusty clothes. 'We would have put on our party outfits.'

'It's not a party,' said Nancy. 'Those are just the workmen's cars!'

Of course this was more than sixty years ago, when workmen in Ireland just didn't have cars. They either walked or cycled, often miles, to get to work. Suddenly we felt that we were, indeed, in a foreign country. The house was very "grand", with tall pillars forming a great porch. We were reminded of the big houses back home that had been burnt down in the "troubles".

Meanwhile we were playing a tournament match every day, and were not doing too badly. We beat Wales and tied with Scotland, but were soundly beaten by England who took their hockey seriously. They had dieted, and exercised, and stayed "dry" both on the sea-journey out and in New York. They were never defeated. I think we also lost to the American team even though they were new to hockey. There were South African and Australian teams - eight in all. I can't remember all the details, but I do remember having a wonderful time.

When we went on tour we won all our games. We were even asked to coach one or two of the various college teams we met. I didn't know where to start. I had been playing hockey for ages, but never examined how or why I did so. I just played for fun and was now expected to teach others! We all did our best to sound authoritative, and were "tickled pink" by the great respect in which we were held (not that we had really earned it).

After the tournament we had a sightseeing day when we were taken south to Washington DC, and to George Washington's own beautiful residence. It was built in an attractive Southern style, and looked warm and homely. Then we were given a wonderful lunch, courtesy of a local millionaire, in a large hall decorated with all the heads of the big game he or his father had shot all round the world. Afterwards there was a dance laid on for us, but it fell a bit flat as we were an overwhelmingly big bunch of females and there were very few men to dance with! I did have a dance with our attractive,

DINNER

GIVEN BY

THE ANCHOR LINE

TO

THE SCOTTISH WOMEN'S HOCKEY PARTY

Captain :

Miss J. A Bryce	St. Andrews

Team Members :

Miss J. R. Caird	Edinburgh
Miss J. H. Stannard	Glasgow
Miss B. B. Moffat	Milngavie
Miss E. A. Munro	Edinburgh
Miss A. Forrester	St. Andrews
Miss E McKerrow	Dumfries
Miss M. S. Fisher	Edinburgh
Miss M. C. Henderson	Glasgow
Miss E. Walker	Glasgow

Delegates :

Miss J. Macqueen, *Hon. Secy.*, S.W.H.A.	Glasgow
Miss S. A. Scott *Hon. Treas.*, S.W.H.A.	St. Andrews
Miss D. S. Holmes	Berwick

Visitors :

Miss E. Campbell	Edinburgh
Miss K. Fairbairn	Edinburgh
Miss J. E. Crabbie	Edinburgh

THE IRISH WOMEN'S HOCKEY PARTY

Manager :

Miss I. Brandon	Belfast

Vice-Captain :

Miss K. M. Kirkwood	Lisburn

Team Members :

Miss C. C. Parsons	Dublin
Miss I. Young	Holywood
Miss D. Ennis	Dublin
Miss J. R. Harman	Queenstown
Miss C. Symes	Galway
Miss L. Hutton	Dublin
Mrs. E. D. M. Findlater	Dublin
Miss J. F. Croome	Clonmel

Delegate :

Miss M. Lehane	Cork

Visitor :

Miss M. J. McKeown	Antrim

Wishing you All every Success
and Happy Memories

Part of the commemorative menu card given to us by the Captain and crew of the SS Cameronia *(1936).*

but very shy, host and felt it was a "feather in my cap". We all had the idea on the way out of picking up a millionaire husband, but this was the nearest I got to it!

Then it was back to New York where we made the most of our second short stay. We fitted in a visit to the *Ziegfield Follies*, and one of my postcards home read "Tomorrow we shop, then play New York Hockey team, then swim in Fordham College pool. Then dine, then either the theatre or Horse-Show." We didn't waste any time!

After New York we had another match in Providence, Rhode Island, and a final one in Boston, Massachusetts. Then we were picked up by the *SS Cameronia* of the same Anchor Line which had brought us out.

Four busy weeks had flashed by, but we felt we were different people going home. America has that effect on people, and makes them grow up quickly. The Americans had planned it all so well, and had been so very kind to us. Now the *SS Cameronia* crew topped it all by giving us, and the Scottish team, a wonderful farewell banquet. They put several tables together to make a long one shaped like a hockey stick. Each of us was given a special menu card as a keepsake, on which was announced the "Piping of the Haggis". This was performed with all solemnity by a kilted piper who marched all round the long table. The only thing they didn't plan for was for the weather to take a hand. We had all just received our portions of haggis, when an extra large wave hit the ship, the table tilted and the haggis all went sliding down to the lower end! Fortunately, amid much laughter, our Irish goalie managed to field them all before they hit the deck!!

Next day, we sailed into Belfast Harbour and, amid many goodbyes and promises to keep in touch, went home to tell our families all about our trip of a lifetime.

Turning Point

Some people remember things so clearly, but I can't because my memory is so bad. Looking back, there are blank periods of which I can recall nothing. Every now and then something stands out like a pillar in the fog. Something joyful, or surprising, or more often something frightening or painful which continues to hurt to this very day.

I can usually remember the turning points, but what took me from radiography at the Children's Hospital to the Gate Theatre is all extremely vague. I think it was performing with the amateur drama group in the Unitarian Church in Stephen's Green that made me want to do more. Also my mother knew the Moores, in particular Meriel Moore, one of the Gate Theatre company. She it was who put me in touch with Hilton Edwards and Mícheál MacLiammoir and arranged for me to join the Gate School of Acting. When some of my mother's friends told her that she shouldn't allow me to join a company run by two homosexuals, she replied 'And why not? I think she'll be safer there than anywhere else!' More power to her, I thought, and I was to find out that she was right. Hilton and Mícheál were two of the kindest and most reliable people that I was ever to meet in my experience of theatre management.

Hilton seemed to manage the business side of things. I think he was the first to bring modern lighting skills to Dublin. I was fascinated by his lighting rehearsals, which he held with only the stage electrician. Later on, I was sorry that I hadn't asked him to teach me more about it when I was there. I could see for myself that it wasn't always necessary to change the scenery. Just a change of lighting focussed on a different part of the stage could transport the audience. After all, it hadn't been such a long time since stage lighting depended upon footlights alone. In addition, Hilton not only produced, directed and lit a play, but he also played one of the important characters - indeed, sometimes the lead. As a result, he often had difficulty in learning his lines, something he always left to the very last moment.

Mícheál was very handsome with a wonderful profile, which Hilton was able to exploit to the full. On stage, Mícheál had invented his own character. He appeared to be a native Irishman complete with the Gaelic language in which, with great industry and perseverance, he had made himself fluent. In reality, he was only half Irish, and rejoiced in the name of Alfred Wilmore. He was born in London. Some people called him "the broth of a boy" on stage, but off it he was a charming, genuine person. He was very talented artistically. He designed and created the scenery for each production. He also designed the costumes with the help of the Wardrobe Mistress. In addition, he wrote a play entitled *Ill Met By Moonlight* in which he played the leading part. I remember well the stream of moonlight provided by Hilton, flooding in from the wings and illuminating his famous profile.

For me it was very hard work. It meant working in the hospital every morning - it had always been a part-time job - and going on to the Gate Theatre in the afternoon. Sometimes, I had to attend in the evening as well if we were required for crowd-work, or for a small speaking part. 'That's what they ran the school for!' said one friend. 'They got you to pay them for the small parts instead of the other way round!' I understood this to be true, but realised that it was the only way they could afford to give us these wonderful plays, properly produced and complete with all the necessary crowd-work. For me it was a start, and I loved every minute of it.

For once, my memory is crystal clear about watching my first professional dress rehearsal. It was Eugene O'Neill's *Mourning Becomes Electra*, and the rehearsal went on into the early morning hours. I can't remember much about our crowd-work, but I was able to sit in the darkened auditorium watching Hilton produce and the cast struggling with their costumes and the new scenery. Hilton stopped them time and time again as he modified his lighting, or "bellowed" for Mícheál to come from the faraway scenery-dock to alter, or add to, the scenery which he had created.

At one stage, Coralie Carmichael, in a wonderfully long, clinging, green velvet dress, stopped in mid-speech to say 'Hilton, I can't act in this bloody awful DRESS!'

Hilton comforted her, demonstrating the great patience with which he addressed every problem. 'It looks magnificent, darling. We'll just get it lifted a bit there and then you won't trip.'

I admired the sheer dedication of the whole company, to go on until they got it right, even if that was just before the time when the first night audience would begin to arrive. They would still perform regardless. It didn't matter if they had eaten, it didn't matter if they had slept - the show went on to the best of their ability. It was an atmosphere so different from that in which I'd lived up until then, where people counted their working hours, got regular meals and enough sleep. At that time, I hadn't realised that the theatre was so crowded and that the real problem was finding employment. There were three or four people competing for every job. I was happy in my ignorance for the time being.

A lot of crowd-work came our way in *Peer Gynt*, with many changes of costume. It was, and is, a wonderful play with music that I love. I was particularly moved by Aase's death scene which I watched from the wings every night with tears in my eyes. I had learned Solveig's beautiful song some time before, but could never hit the soft top note with which it finishes. It was just sheer nerves - they crippled me. They still do!

In due course, in late 1937, I was given a small speaking part in one of the productions and was thrilled to bits. It was my first professional part and everyone was very complimentary about it. But my stage-voice was very under-developed, and Hilton said 'Louise, just shout and that will be just right!' Then one day Dr. Collis, one of the consultants to the Children's Hospital, arrived with his play about the Dublin slums called *Marrowbone Lane*. He found me sitting in the auditorium and recognised me as the Children's Hospital radiographer. He had taken great interest in my doings there with regard to the X-ray department. Anyway, the long and the short of it was that he offered me a small part in his play. "Nepotism", I suppose you would call it, but I was so delighted to play a nursing sister in the short hospital scene that I didn't think about it. I don't think Hilton or anyone else held it against me.

Most afternoons, Coralie Carmichael or Meriel Moore would give us classes in acting, which they fitted in between their own rehearsals. They would set us speeches to learn. They taught us how to break up these speeches and then to add movement. But I think it was the actual performances under Hilton's direction that taught me most. Anyway it seems that I was a "natural". My main difficulty throughout my theatre days was this poor memory of mine, never properly exercised since the time when I was doing exams. It always

Pygmalion, *by George Bernard Shaw, The Gate Theatre (1937). Coralie Carmichael and Mícheál MacLiammoir are centre left. I am third from the right, in my first ever crowd scene.*

made learning my lines a struggle and it was, in the end, to defeat me.

Some people can learn their lines independently of the movements that are only given later at rehearsal. I really needed the moves before I learned the lines, and to practise them together until they became solid. We often didn't get the time to do it this way, and I could seldom make the most of longer parts in which I was just getting good by the time the play was due to come off! I remember taking minor comfort from watching Betty Chancellor rehearsing a speech into which Hilton had just put new moves. Time and time again she tried to match them and failed. Hilton would watch and say, 'Try it again, darling,' until suddenly she got it and never lost it again.

Meanwhile, I was burning the candle at both ends and got sinusitis so badly that I had to have a very painful operation on my nose. There was no penicillin in those days. The operation was performed by the hospital ENT - Ear, Nose and Throat - consultant entirely free of charge. I was still regarded as hospital staff, although I never went back there after a rather slow recovery. So slow, in fact, that my mother and I realised I couldn't do both hospital and theatre. My mother was glad to have me stay at home and so I had no difficulty in making up my mind which one to give up.

The theatre had become my life.

You Can't Take It With You, *Gaiety Theatre (1938).*
I am on the left, playing Essie.

The Gate Theatre

The first year had flown past and I spent the second year also at the Gate School, ostensibly under-studying Coralie and Meriel. It was my own suggestion in order to justify staying on at the school. Actually, it was a "bit of a cod" on my part, as I never paid any real attention to how Coralie or Meriel did their speeches, but it kept me going and hopefully Hilton would recognise my potential.

However, as an experienced professional, he could see that I really wasn't under-studying at all. If Coralie or Meriel had become ill I wouldn't have been able to walk on in their place. He broke it to me gently that there would be no place for me in the company at that time. One of the students who started with me had married his stage-manager. Also Mícheál's niece, Sally Travers, would tour with them and would share any small parts, with the result that nothing would be left for me. I could see the point and retired gracefully, but asked for his advice.

He suggested that Anew McMaster, Mícheál's brother-in-law, might have an opening for me, as one member of his touring company was planning to retire. They very kindly arranged an audition for me. But I was soon to find out that Anew, or "Mac" as his company knew him, was difficult to pin down. I remember my irritation after travelling out to the far end of Howth, with difficulty finding his cottage at the very "back of beyond", only to find out that he wasn't there! But I kept on trying and finally did meet him at the Gate Theatre, and did a speech, or read a part - I can't remember now.

He was kind, but vague, and he said that I could join his company 'probably next month'. He would get in touch with me. I was delighted and thought it was all fixed, but ... the lady in question never left and kept on doing one more part for him. Again and again I was told 'Next month, darling, for sure.' It was agony! At this stage, I had no hospital job, and couldn't look for theatre work if I was going to join his company "next month"! Believe it or not, this went on for six months. It seemed an age to me with nothing to do, so finally I wrote and told him that I wouldn't wait any longer and was going to look for other work.

I've wondered ever since should I have gone on waiting? The actress I should have been replacing did actually leave the company in the autumn of 1938. When she got back to Dublin, she rang me up to inform me and to ask me why had I given up? By that time, I was rehearsing a very small part with a rather inferior crowd. Anyway my pride was hurt and I felt explosive, and so I wrote an indignant letter to Hilton and Mícheál about how badly I had been treated. With hindsight I know that was silly. They had done their best for me and probably knew their Anew. I never did get a reply. They just didn't want to know.

Mac was such a "character" that I should have known what to expect. Six months! Why, that was nothing in comparison with missing such an opportunity. I would have learnt so much from him. McMaster was theatre personified - and so was this my first big mistake? It suited him to have me in reserve, and it saved him and his company from having extra rehearsals. Why didn't I go and see him and his company perform where ever they were in the west of Ireland? It was partly on account of the money involved. I didn't feel I should waste it on a non-paid trip now that I wasn't earning anything. A year or two later I would have been more flexible. Maybe I could have helped with stage management and have got started understudying (properly this time) the parts I was to take over. Anew was well-known for his Shakespearean parts, and he would have built up my feeble voice and my self confidence.

Of course, it's easy to see clearly with hindsight. I felt very low and defeated, and I knew that I shouldn't have accepted the small part I was rehearsing. This company had promised me a good part, but they never let me know that they had given it to someone else until the day that we met to rehearse. I was so anxious to have something to show McMaster that I let them get away with it.

I was feeling victimised when my sister-in-law, Raydene, came to visit and wrote the following poem for me:

Ode to a Sausage

There was an old lout called McMaster
Who wanted Louise and he asked her
To go on a tour,
Beginning May four,
But alas on that date he just passed her.

This same stupid Anew McMaster
Told Charlotte Louise he had cast her
For parts small and great,
That might lead to the Gate,
If she worked just a little bit faster.

Miss Hutton who doubted McMaster
Consulted with W.A.A.M.A. who grasped her*
Just in time from this lout,
Whose contracts no doubt,
Were worth less than an old-fashioned plaster!

* (Actor's Trade Union at that time)

This made me laugh so much in the midst of disaster that I've carried a copy of it in my handbag ever since, and take it out when needed like smelling salts! Once you can laugh at yourself you've started recovering, and sure enough my luck changed and I got the part of "Essie", a young balletomane, in *You Can't Take It With You*. This was a play which was put on at the Gaiety Theatre in Dublin, with a pleasant producer and company. I thoroughly enjoyed it and made some good friends.

I also started broadcasting with the RTE Repertory Company, at that time still on the top floor of the GPO. It had been rebuilt after being badly damaged during the Easter 1916 rebellion. Larry Morrow had given me an audition and was such an expert on voices that he correctly placed mine as half Scottish. My mother came from Glasgow, and for once my "feeble" voice was an asset and very suitable for broadcasting. I loved working with him. He was such a good producer.

There I met people with whom I would be touring later on in the Carl Clopet Company - a real "Fit-Up" as these companies were called. It was a wonderful experience, to travel the highways and byways of Northern Ireland with such a happy company. I'll never forget it and if you like I will share it with you now.

This is one of a set of general publicity photographs which we would have sent around to producers and agents, looking for parts (1947).

Fit Up

I can't remember exactly how I got on this tour around Northern Ireland, in spring 1939, but as several friends from the Gaiety Theatre show *You Can't Take It With You* were also there, it must have followed on from that. I can't remember it all in detail, but my first "digs" I can remember perfectly.

The first thing a "Fit-up" company does on arrival in a town is to find somewhere to sleep that night. Theatrical "digs" are an experience in themselves. They are usually quite unpretentious, in fact invisible to everybody apart from those who have been there before, or who have studied the list of addresses at the theatre. The first one I tried was located in Newry, County Armagh.

We arrived at a little paper shop with a few bundles of newspapers thrown on to a "tatty" wooden counter. My heart sank at the sight of it, but when we were shown into the cosy little house out back, it lifted again. There was a neat, tiled kitchen with an open stove and comfortable chairs, and a great warm welcome from our hostess. She already knew all about the Carl Clopet Company, but she wanted to know what plays we were putting on, and who was playing which parts? Then she asked 'What would you like for your tea, dear?' and 'When will you be home for supper?'

We got full board for about £2 to £3 in those days, which was amazing value. Our host families knew exactly what our salaries were worth and that we couldn't afford any more. They loved the theatre and theatre-folk, and moreover were quite used to supplying any props - big or small - that we required. These included quite sizeable items of furniture which would be delivered to the theatre for us. That was how the "Fit-ups" got their name in the first place.

We carried curtains rather than scenery, and the people came not only to see us perform, but also to see how their own "bits and pieces" looked on stage. Then they would discuss it all with us after the show, over the good solid supper they would hurry home to cook for us.

So, after finding our digs, the next job was to search out these props and get them along to the theatre. The play was Daphne du Maurier's *Rebecca*, for which I was understudying the leading role as well as having my own small part. My special job was to visit the biggest bank, or school, where there might be a collection of silver cups or trophies, and to ask for a loan of them. Then I had to ask for some flowers from somebody with a garden, and to arrange them as best I could in the biggest silver cup or vase. I remember running over my understudy lines whilst doing all this, and wondering whether I would ever be able to cope if asked to perform.

All this pre-show activity relating to the props was great publicity for the company, and let everybody know that we were there and what the play was about. Indeed, one summer afternoon in Derry, a group of us were walking up the main street carrying a fine collection of silver trophies, when we were stopped by the police who wanted to know where we had got all the treasures we were carrying and what we were going to do with it! We managed to reassure them about our intentions and, into the bargain, made them promise to come and see the show that very night!

I must admit that we met with one or two very poor housekeepers on this tour, the worst being at Fintona, a little market town near Omagh in County Tyrone. This town rejoiced in having the only horse-drawn tram that I had ever seen, let alone travelled in! It took us from Omagh to Fintona in about half an hour, and I was fascinated to watch from the front seat of the upper deck how this great big elderly horse was able to pull this great big elderly tram along the original tram-lines. There were several places where branch lines joined in, but he was able to negotiate the points by placing his great big hairy hooves in the right spot without moderating his steady trot. Sometimes, he actually crossed his legs as in a well-practised dance.

We enjoyed this short journey immensely but, when we arrived in Fintona, it was to find a big market day in progress and digs correspondingly scarce. So "Mrs. Danvers" and I had to take what was available and we ended up with only a lumpy double bed between us. We thought we were tired enough to sleep anyway, but soon after lights out we felt uncomfortable, and putting them on again discovered that we were beset by a hungry flock of fleas! I started to catch some of them, but my companion found it very difficult, having fashionably long, red-lacquered nails. She could only pounce on one, then look helplessly at me and ask 'Louise, what do I do next?' This made us laugh so much that we gave up. We spent the rest of the night sitting up wrapped in our coats and top blankets, and next morning managed to book in at the only hotel, where the Clopets and the leading actress and actor were already installed.

After this, we did some sea-side places including Ballycastle in County Antrim where we socialised with some of the British army stationed nearby. They came in to see the show, and were glad to come round afterwards for a drink and a chat at the local pub. I think that they were finding time to be heavy on their hands. I took a great liking to one of the officers, who was nick-named "Jumbo", and he promised to get in touch when next he was on leave and we were back home. Of course, he never did and I was torn in twain between thinking that perhaps he wasn't allowed to come down to the rebellious south, and the suspicion that he already had a wife and family back in England!

The next stop was Derry. We were booked in for three days, and so had an opportunity to stop and think for the first time during this tour, and to do a little shopping. We had almost full houses every night. I never got the opportunity to play the lead, but in a way was just as glad not to have the responsibility given my unreliable memory. It is strange looking back now, how little I remember of the Clopets. They didn't really mix with the company, and usually booked into hotels or stayed with friends.

Suddenly, it was our last date which was at Trim, County Meath. There three of us decided that we were so near to Dublin that we wouldn't look for digs, and instead we hired three bicycles and rode them home after the show. I was sad to say goodbye, and nobody seemed to know what they would be doing next. We set off immediately after our performance. It was a truly beautiful, moonlit night. I have a vivid picture in my mind of Trim with its great curved castle wall and battlements, bathed in the bright moonlight, as we pedalled away round it to join the Dublin road and our own uncertain futures.

A Hallow-E'en Game

My story starts with the Knave of Hearts -
That handsome chap who stole the tarts
Which were baked by the beauteous Queen of Hearts
For the King just home from foreign parts.

When she fell a-weeping, the Knave came creeping
To tell her he was sorry.
For he loved the Queen more than passing well
And he told her not to worry.
'Alas!' she cried, 'It's lost I am,
I can't make more for we're out of jam!'
'Then come my love, we'd better flee
Away, away across the sea .....!'

But the Queen (a trifle vain was she)
Said 'Just a minute, while I pack.'
So the King caught the Knave
And with one great whack
He cut off the head of this luckless Jack
And put it where the tarts had been
As a warning to all - but specially his Queen.

When she went to cook she took one look
And passed out clean!
Since when she's never again been seen
Save her sad little ghost at Hallow-E'en!

Now the Queen of Spades in towering passion
(For she loved the Knave in her own dark fashion),
Began to plot revenge.
And she was a witch - a terrible witch.

She cast a spell, a shrinking spell,
And she worked so hard
That she shrank the King
To the size of a card
And all who tried to help him as well
Such was the strength of this dangerous spell!

All save two: the King of Diamonds was one
And the Ace of Clubs who was his Prime Minister
(Second to none but a trifle sinister).
But the King didn't trust him, no not he,
So he made him an Admiral 'n sent him to sea!

Now this King was in his counting house
Counting out his money.
He didn't know what had happened
But he thought the silence funny.
So he called upon his Joker to tell him the news:
'We must put this wicked Witch to death -
There's no time to lose!'
The King said 'How'll we do it?
So that her spell won't shrink me too?'
For he knew that the Joker was more than his Fool -
Some said the Devil
But a mighty Magician at either level!
And he told the King
'Just hold my hand and there'll be no hitch.'
So they planned to bury this nasty old Witch,
Holding one hand they each dug the hole
In lumps as dark as her black soul.

But the King had a cold and he had to let go
His nose to blow - 'Oh Woe, Oh Woe!
In a trice he had shrunk to the size of a poker!
But catching again the hand of the Joker
(He didn't give in, he finished the job)
And they put her in, right up to her chin!

Now - You just have to find a card at every scene
And bless your pile of coal this Hallow-E'en!

Sailing Adventure

I can't remember who introduced me to sailing but it wasn't long thereafter that I bought a "Wag". This is a small sailing boat, approximately fourteen feet long with two main sails, and a spinnaker for use on those occasions when one is running before a following wind. It generally takes two people to sail it. There were quite a number of Wags in Dún Laoghaire when I started. I renamed mine "Sprite", under which name I'm told it is still sailing to this day. We used to meet on Wednesday evenings to race in the harbour, and

Sailing Sprite in Dún Laoghaire harbour (1938).

on Saturday afternoons to venture outside, weather permitting. We had an experienced sailor in Dickie Pilkington, our captain of the Wags, to make these important decisions.

Wags, although not decked in, are very safe in rough water. I think there is nothing to equal the feeling of silent empowerment when the sails are filled with wind driving the boat along. Of course, I began as crew and had to learn where to put my weight to balance the boat and how to put up the spinnaker. It was only when I got my own boat that I rather shakily took the tiller. Thankfully, I had a very knowledgeable crewman to start with who was able to advise me on some of the finer details!

So all went well for a while. Then came the time when he had to leave Ireland and I found it difficult to find a replacement. Someone told me that Dr. Bertie Corbet, the well-known gynaecologist, had been asking how he could start sailing. Although I was thoroughly nervous I made myself go and see him at Fitzwilliam Place, where all the well-known doctors had their private practices. He welcomed me, and said, 'I'd love to sail with you.'

I said, 'Perhaps you don't realise that although I have a boat, I've had very little experience of taking the tiller, in fact of sailing in general!'

'It doesn't really trouble me,' he replied. 'You see, I'm a long distance swimmer, and could probably rescue the two of us if put to it!'

So began a partnership which lasted his lifetime, and which survived quite a few emergencies. I'd like to tell you about one of these.

There was to be a race for Wags at Howth one particular Saturday in July, and those wanting to compete decided to get there on the previous Wednesday evening when Dublin bay was calm enough. I remember it was a beautiful summer evening with a light breeze. A bit too light as we later found out. Quite a number of Wags set out together with Dickie leading, and we had no doubts about being able to keep up with all the others. But as usual, we fell behind.

When we got near the head of Howth the wind dropped almost completely. The boats ahead of us still had enough wind to get round the head, but suddenly we found that we weren't making any progress. This remained the case even when we dropped the main-sail and got the oars out. Howth has quite a broad, rocky head although it looks narrower looking from Dublin. The tide started running against us, so that row as we might (and the oars were very heavy) we weren't moving forwards. Indeed, we appeared to be moving backwards! It was very frightening as all the other boats had distanced themselves away ahead of us, and were unaware of our predicament.

Bertie suggested that we should go in close to shore and sure enough we found the tide much less strong there. We found we could make some progress, but only slowly and it was beginning to get dark. I was already picking out places among the rocks where we might be able to run the boat ashore, but we turned one more corner and saw lights ahead of us. We also heard the welcome sound of Dickie shouting from the pier, 'Ahoy there Sprite!' When we shouted back he told us how to get into Howth harbour, though in the dark we missed the mooring buoys and ended up aground on the bank at the back of the harbour. Dickie came and picked us up. He was very relieved as he had been just about to row out to look for us.

He wasn't able to pull the boat off, and we decided to leave it where it was until the next day. Dickie took us ashore and very glad I was to be on terra firma again. Fortunately, Bertie had left his car in Howth the day before. I phoned my Mum to tell her we were safe, and that we would be home about midnight. I asked her to prepare some supper for us as we were very hungry.

She said, 'I'm no cook, what shall I do?'

'There's some cold meat in the fridge,' I said. 'Just cook a few spuds and a few garden peas.'

'I don't know how to cook spuds and peas,' said my poor Mum, which set us off laughing all the way home.

When we got to Foxrock we found the peas boiling merrily, and my Mum standing over them trying to push them under water!

So ended our sailing adventure. We were able to take part in the next Saturday's racing at Howth. We were fortunate that the fine weather held for us all to sail home together - and I mean together - on the next day which was Sunday.

Happiness

Happiness spreads like the butter or jam
        We put on our daily bread.
Mine starts with my dog's plumey tail
        As she sings me out of bed.

When the jealous cat circumvents the dog
        Curling up on my lap to sleep,
Her purring pleasure permeates
        And I forget to weep.

A courting couple came into the yard -
        Their happiness radiated.
I remembered the hand I used to hold
        And the joy which it created.

My stricken cousin fights disease
        And laughs when she is troubled.
When I laugh with her each fuels the other
        And healing is then doubled

For laughter is catching like happiness,
        It increases with the giving.
The more we give the more we have
        A positive way of living.

London

I never really planned to join the war effort - like so many things in my life it just sort of happened. In early summer 1940, I was travelling home by train from the city centre to Foxrock, when I met an old friend. He told me that his sister couldn't get home from England for a holiday, because she couldn't find anybody to replace her. As chance would have it, she was a radiographer like myself.

'That's hard,' I said. 'Has she tried over here? There are plenty of people out of work. Myself for instance, although I've only worked with children.'

'If you've X-rayed children successfully you can X-ray anyone,' said my friend eagerly. 'Would you go?'

I hesitated - this was all very sudden. I had been deeply troubled about Irish neutrality for some time, although I still defended it as I had never allowed myself to understand the full implications of what Hitler had planned. It was difficult at the time to know what to believe - how much was propaganda and how much the truth. Before the war started, I had actually admired Hitler and what he seemed to be achieving in Germany. Now I realised that if the Germans got into England, Ireland would be the next stop and I could imagine them goose-stepping up O'Connell Street! We understood enough by this time to know that the man never kept a promise in his life. Here was a great opportunity to go and see for myself.

Suddenly I knew I wanted to go. When my offer was made and accepted, I was full of excitement and also some relief. I was without a job and my love-life had gone very wrong of late. It would be good to get away for a while. Bridie and Lizzie would continue to look after my mother, and anyway it was 'Only for a fortnight' as I told her. Little did we know that the fortnight would stretch out into five years, such was the demand for locums while the war lasted.

I was soon on my way to war-torn England and passed safely over the submarine-laden Irish Sea. As a matter of fact, I don't think the Mail Boat was ever attacked. Then we had to survive a long, exhausting queue at Holyhead while they sorted out passports and travel permits. We had to stand, pushing our hand luggage along in front of us, on a draughty pier for hours on end, and then take whatever train was available heading for London. Even so, I was surprised that there seemed to be so little evidence of war, apart from the careful blackout at night at my first locum. It was a small hospital about 20 miles south of London, although I've forgotten the name. As soon as I arrived my friend's sister showed me "the ropes", and then she left. I was glad to have some quiet time to myself to get accustomed to the X-ray exposure levels required for adults.

After nightfall, it was a different atmosphere altogether. The tension grew as we listened to the sound of heavy aircraft passing overhead. Some we took to be our own aircraft setting out to bomb German targets. The deep concerted drone of many engines, like the bass notes of a great organ, stirred strange atavistic feelings within me - a mixture of fear and elation. Hearing them and not seeing them, I had a picture in my mind of each small team of highly trained people in their tiny pools of carefully screened light, each person intent on his own individual task. They would be working hard to maintain their exact position in this mighty aerial armada. From the comparative safety of the ground below our prayers went with them, wishing each a safe return.

Others we heard, coming the other way, we knew to be German as soon as the London anti-aircraft guns opened up, and we could watch the powerful searchlights criss-crossing the night sky picking out aerial targets for them. On these occasions, it was impossible not to be caught up in the excitement of the moment and to cheer when we scored a hit. Later in the calm time following the "All Clear", one realised that it was similarly brave men both defending and attacking.

At that time, we never appreciated that one of the decisive battles of the war was being being fought over our heads. This was the "Battle of Britain" which pitched "the few" of the RAF Fighter Command against the might of the German Luftwaffe. The aircrews must have been pushed to the end of their strength, and they knew better than most how nearly they were defeated.

I'm no pacifist. I believe that everyone has the right to defend his home or his country. But how does it start? How far back should one go? Perhaps, in the first instance, the German people were too law-abiding and it never occurred to them to question their own government - until it was too late. I had travelled quite a bit in Germany with my hockey team a year or so before *Kristallnacht*, when the *pogrom* against the Jews became widespread. The families with whom we stayed warned us that it was already dangerous to air our views in public. They were ordinary people, just like us, but they were already powerless to alter the flow of events. They couldn't risk their own families being taken away in the dead of the night. I began to be glad that we have never been without rebels here in Ireland. Bad as they often are, they would never tolerate a dictator!

Soon after my arrival in England, I was approached by the Society of Radiographers to enquire if I would be prepared to do other locums after my present one finished. There was such a dearth of radiographers, and so many overworked, weary ones who needed a break, that I hadn't the heart to say 'No'. In due course I was looking for "digs" in London proper, and was lucky enough to find a bed-sitter in Earls Court, West London. This was located in a semi-basement, and I was glad of this fact on my first night which happened to coincide with the last big bombing raid on London. As I lay there, quaking in my newly-found bed, I listened first to the fearsome sound of the sirens wailing their warning, followed by the "crump, crump" of the heavy explosions, which seemed to be coming nearer and nearer every minute. Then I heard the chatter of our own anti-aircraft guns responding. I was slightly comforted by the knowledge that I was already partly underground, and that only a direct hit would bring the house down on top of me. Even then, they might be able to dig down to find me still warm in my bed!

Truly, it was a memorable night. London's marvellous defenders were stretched to their utmost - guncrews, searchlight operators (many of whom were women), firefighters, ambulance crews, emergency diggers working frantically - some in the ruins of their own houses; electricity and water engineers, trying to restore lighting and to stem floods; London Underground railway workers who ventured out to find people and bring them into the safety of "the tube". These were supported by the ordinary Londoners, who gathered with their families each night in these tunnels, bringing bedding and food and their indomitable good spirits, and expansive generosity one to another. No wonder there was a lull after this last great bombardment, as the Germans counted their losses - very heavy losses - and planned a different way to break London's spirit.

Obviously, this plan was already in the pipeline, and I was there when the first flying bombs, or "doodle-bugs" as they were called, started to arrive. By then, I had changed my "digs" and was living in a back street quite close to Euston Station. I used to visit the station sometimes when I felt homesick. It comforted me just to hear the Irish voices all around, especially when the Irish Mail was due to leave. Euston was a prime target, of course, but I had developed a sort of fatalism by then. 'If it's going to get me, it's going to get me!' And it worked - I stopped worrying.

I had a room on the fourth floor of one of a row of houses, all with dormer windows opening onto the sloping roofs. We felt quite safe to watch as long as we could hear these tiny pilotless planes approaching, and flying on past us. Many were quite low enough for us to see them as we all leaned out of our dormer windows on both sides of the street. But then the engine would stop abruptly, which meant it was about to drop and explode on contact. As if carefully rehearsed, all the windows slammed shut at the same moment, and I would dive under the bed and hope for the best! Our road never sustained a direct hit, but the doodle-bugs stretched our nerves all the same.

I was still in London when the V2 rockets arrived. As it happened, I was standing in a crowd of people at Hyde Park corner listening to one of the speakers on his soap-box. Suddenly, this "thing" arrived without warning out of a clear, blue sky. There was a huge explosion. With hindsight, we knew that it wasn't very near to us, but the entire crowd went silent and every man, woman and child lay down flat - me among them! I'd never seen a crowd do that before. As nothing further happened, we all got up again and started talking about it. These V2s were the worst of all because we got no warning whatsoever, but thankfully there weren't very many of them. This resulted from the fact that Hitler had bragged repeatedly about his secret weapon which would pulverise London, and we would learn later on that the RAF had searched out many of the launching sites and destroyed them before they could be used.

By this time, I had given up any idea of retreating home as long as I was of some use. I could now appreciate what we in Ireland never realised, which was how near to defeat London, and indeed Britain, had been. It had never occurred to us that the mighty British could really lose this war, even after Dunkirk. We had been inspired by all the little boats which went to bring their men off the beaches. Now that I understood this, and how tired and hardpressed they were, I couldn't leave. I had a steady job in an old hospital in the centre of London, and I stayed there until the Normandy landings took place and the end of the war was in sight.

Then it was that I worked my way back into the theatre again - but that's another story.

The Misses Bruce - Eliza, Jane, Charleten and Susan (early 1900s). I'm not certain which one is the visiting cousin - perhaps you can tell?

Scotland The Brave

This morning there was a big black spider in the bath and I shuddered as I knew I would have to rescue it again. I've rescued it so many times before I feel I know him (or her) personally. Anyway, my mother was a Robertson, a clan which can claim direct descent from Robert the Bruce. As everyone knows, he was so inspired by a persistent spider when on the point of giving up the struggle, that he returned to the fight and at Bannock Burn drove the English out of Scotland for a very long time. So, no true Scot will ever kill a spider. Actually, I'm connected to Robert twice over. Once through Robert Hutton, a distant cousin who was directly connected back to the time when Robert the Bruce was King of Scotland in 1306, and again through the Bruces of Northern Ireland.

I only knew of the last members of that family - three old ladies, all centenarians. I was told that when some one tried to sympathise with the last old lady on the death of her sisters, all she would say was 'Now at last I can have a room of my own!'

But why does this spider keep on falling into my bath? Why does it make the same mistake over and over again? Does it lose its way in the dark, or does it have a poor memory - like me? Perhaps this is my Irish spider's message: that I must not only keep a diary but remember to read it as well! I've missed out on so many special dates, one of my worst lapses being in Scotland, soon after joining the Glasgow Citizens' Theatre in summer 1945.

I had been very lucky to have been given an introduction to James Bridie, the well known Scottish playwright, at a time when he, together with Matthew Forsyth, the new director, were planning a season which included an Irish play. This was followed by an experimental play of Bridie's own with many scenes and character parts, and I was taken on for a very welcome six month contract. I found very good "digs" with Mrs. Goldie - a well known theatre landlady and supporter of the Citizens' - and began to enjoy life in general.

The Citizens' had the disadvantage of being situated in a very bad part of Glasgow, near the docks. This was all to be upgraded in the near future, but it was still dangerous with what were known as "Razor Gangs". We had been well warned, and we never went home by ourselves after dark, but always in a group.

One cold night in midwinter, our group stopped at a "hot-dog" stand and were enjoying the hot food. There followed a sudden silence and Archie Duncan, a Glaswegian, warned us to hurry up and move on and not to look behind us. But some impulsive female had already done so and now screamed, and we realised that we were surrounded by a Razor Gang. We knew them by the vicious scarred faces, and by the menacing silence, and we were glad we had Archie with us that night. He was a great, big, powerful looking fellow who had worked as a rivetter in the ship-building industry before taking up acting. We clustered around him and marched unopposed to the nearest bus-stop. The scarred watchers would not know he was such a kind gentle person, although I'm sure he would have given a good account of himself if put to the test. We never knew if we were the target that night, or whether it was two rival gangs facing each other and establishing their territorial rights, and we didn't wait to find out!

My "digs" were a long bus-ride away from the theatre. Once I got there I tended to "stay put", as I was able to boil a kettle in the green room and make tea and sandwiches between shows on *matinée* days, or during rehearsals. There hadn't been enough money available to make proper dressing rooms, when the theatre was being done up, but there was plenty of space available backstage for two big open dressing rooms. From there a long passage-way led down to the old stage-door, and its elderly guardian Alistair McCurtain ... yes, *McCurtain*. He was rather sensitive about it and we learned not to labour the point. I think he came with the original theatre and felt it belonged to him, and he would "tick us off" if we were late. At the other end of the line was Matthew Forsyth, in his office at the front of the house near the booking office. He had just come out of the army and also demanded punctuality. Although kindly, he seemed rather like a schoolmaster which did not suit some of the old hands.

One day, when I thought I was free, I went shopping in the

afternoon, and turned up at the theatre about four o'clock in order to make myself a cup of tea. As I came in at the stage door I noticed Alistair's face - it was a "study" as he picked up the phone and announced my arrival. I was amazed, but all he would say excitedly was 'It's the interval now - it's the interval!'

A moment later, the entire cast came running down the passageway crying out 'Where have you been?' and 'Are you alright?'

Archie, in particular, gave me a big hug and said, 'I was afraid you were in an accident.' Looking at my puzzled face, he added, 'It's the *matinée* - you've missed the *matinée*!'

I felt my heart drop into my boots, as I said, 'But that's tomorrow, isn't it? This is Tuesday - isn't it?'

'No,' said someone, 'it's Wednesday. You've lost a day!' and they began to trickle back up the passage-way as bells announced the end of the interval. They could see I was suffering from shock and they were all being very kind, but "the show must go on". Someone even managed to make me a cup of tea! When I asked what they had done, the stage manager told me they had just cut my scene out completely as there were no understudies. He thought the audience might not even have noticed my absence, and I began to feel a little bit better. But then a message came to go and see Matthew Forsyth, in his office, and my knees started to knock uncontrollably. He was very angry, and gave me such a fierce dressing-down that I feared instant dismissal.

I did my best to apologise and told him of my memory problems, and suddenly he relented, saying 'I really ought to fire you - DON'T DO IT AGAIN!' and I survived. Ever afterwards, Alistair always reminded me the night before a *matinée*, and insisted that I tell him when I should be rehearsing. I don't think James Bridie ever knew of my defection - a great relief as he was such a kind, approachable person and I hated to let him down.

When We Are Married, *Guildford Repertory Theatre (1947). I am second from the right, playing Annie Parker. On the extreme right is Anna Wing, who would become famous in later years as the Grandmother in* Eastenders.

Citizens' Theatre

We had a mixed company, with a hard core of local Scots and the rest from over the border. There was Molly Urquhart, a well known Glasgow comedienne, who was so helpful to me when I was trying to acquire a good Scottish accent. There was Archie Duncan, Jimmie Gibson and several others who had acted in the old Princess's Theatre, before it was renamed the Citizens'. We had a new juvenile lead in pretty Rona Anderson from Edinburgh. She was a sweet person who always looked prettier offstage than on, and eventually she made her way into films where she was much more successful. Then we had Douglas Campbell who was my ideal of a young Scot who should always have worn a kilt - but who lived in London - and Richmond Nairn, and David Dawson the tall Australian, and several others. David was much too tall for his own good, as it limited the parts available to him. He became a good friend to me later on when I was in need. It was a friendly company where I felt happy, a point which I didn't fully appreciate at the time.

It was a fortnightly repertory, although sometimes plays lasted three weeks or more which gave me sufficient time to learn my lines. One of my Scottish cousins, Gladys Ruff, a teacher by profession, was living in Glasgow at the time. Luckily for me, she was kind enough to hear my parts over and over until I felt secure. She was also a patron of the Citizens' and never missed a performance. I had a lovely little comic maidservant's part in the play by Paul Vincent Carroll - *The White Steed* - in which Michael Golden from Dublin played the new young priest who tries to reform the older man. The (Irish) heroine has a fascinating scene where she gets so worked up that she attacks the "delft" on the well-filled dresser, and hurls it plate by plate across her kitchen. A most satisfying display, but expensive as new plates had to be supplied for each performance!

My next part was a complete contrast, being that of an old woman of the roads in James Bridie's play, *Lancelot*. I was so delighted when he complimented me on both parts.

I was happy with my parts as I hadn't expected any better, but some of the other newcomers felt they had not been given the parts they had been led to expect, and were discontented. They made no secret of the fact that they would not be staying on when their present contract terminated, after the Christmas pantomime. I suppose I got it into my head that the company would be breaking up at that time. I think this influenced my judgement when, right "out of the blue", a part in a London play was offered to me. It came from the brother of Dr. Robert Collis of *Marrowbone Lane* fame at the Gate Theatre in Dublin. This was Maurice Collis, an expert on the far east, especially of China. He had written a very interesting book about the great Chinese Empress who had ruled for the last fifty years before China became open to the world. Apparently, she was known as "The Motherly and Auspicious". He had now adapted the book and made it into a play which was to be produced by Henry Sherek in the West End of London. Maurice was certain there would be a part in it for me!

I, of course, was vastly flattered and indulged in much wishful thinking, and wrote a letter to James Bridie to tell him about it. I got a really charming letter back, not only saying that he was sorry to lose me, but also offering me an introduction to Henry Sherek. I have kept a copy of this letter for more than fifty years, and I make no apology for quoting it here as it kept me going when times were hard.

It starts *"My dear Henry"* - (and a general introduction follows)

Then he says:

"She is an actress with a pretty wide range and a really remarkable sense of comedy. I think she is likely to make a name for herself in this line, as her attack is excellent and she has a mixture of Scottish and Irish blood, in which the Scots commonsense controls the Irish extravagance! If you can give her a job I think it possible that you may find she is a discovery!

Yours etc.

signed James Mavor" (Bridie's real name)

That should have done the trick but the sad thing was that the play was fated never to be staged, and even I gave up hoping after two or three months. Poor Maurice, a brilliant scholar but new to theatre politics, was devastated, but he had nothing else to offer me. I had arrived in London by that time, and now had no work! With hindsight, I don't think my Scottish commonsense was active when I took such an Irish gamble and left the Citizens'. I should have stayed on there for as long as they had parts for me, and it would have built up confidence and my reputation.

Before I left for London, we all had great fun in the Christmas Pantomime, in which I actually had a part as a Chinese Empress. Perhaps Dr. Mavor had a suspicion that Maurice's play was unlikely to "take off".

Mrs. Goldie, my landlady, was well named. She lived in a typical, grey-faced Glasgow tenement with an open archway entrance and a communal, grey cement staircase. Depressing, surely, but clean. Mrs. Goldie's apartment was one of two on the first landing. When we got back after the evening show she opened the door to us, and the golden light and her personal warmth flooded out from her large and well appointed rooms.

'Come away in. I have your supper ready. How did it all go tonight?'

She kept our supper warm for us in a wall oven, beside the open fire where we would eat most nights. She always wanted to know everything that had happened at the theatre during the day, and as she saw all the shows we welcomed her comments. She had been devastated by my missing of the *matinée* performance, and joined with the several people who now kept me reminded which day it was! She had a very good-looking daughter, with a Dutch boy-friend who was in what remained of the Dutch Navy. When his ship was in we often got the benefit of some special delicacy he had managed to smuggle in - such as extra butter or meat, or pineapples or some other exotic fruit.

Then came Christmas, and as we were all in the Christmas Pantomime we couldn't spend it with our own families. Imagine our surprise when we got back to our "digs" to find a big table laid out in the kitchen, with a wonderful Christmas dinner spread out! She had managed to get a big turkey and some ham. The Dutch sailor had brought every conceivable "Goody" for us, including a pair of silk stockings for each of the ladies! He and his fiancée had waited to eat with us, and a cousin or three as well, and it was a memorable occasion.

I'll never forget the sight of that table, laden down with things

The Chinese Empress, in the Christmas Pantomime, Citizens' Theatre (1945).

almost impossible to get at that time, and lit up with candles and good cheer. It was a real "home from home" and Mrs. Goldie typified Scotland - but especially Glasgow - for me. I rate her the "Queen of all landladies" that ever were!

She Stoops To Conquer, *by Oliver Goldsmith, Children's Theatre (1947).*
I am third from the left, playing Constance. Susan Kennaway is directly behind me.

The Children's Theatre

The phone rang, and a voice said 'Louise? This is Susan.' I didn't recognise the confident, mature voice.

'Susan of the Children's Theatre ...,' she explained, and a flood of memories swept over me.

Susan Kennaway and I had been in the Glyndebourne Children's Theatre in 1947, not long after the war ended. In the intervening years we had met once or twice in London, but it was ages since I had actually talked to her, so now we had a great long chat.

Every year, Susan and her husband went to Glyndebourne for the opera season. Earlier in the year, she had read an article in the programme entitled *Glyndebourne and Children*, to which was added a footnote: "Any comparable material would be warmly welcomed by the archive". Susan explained that she was writing her own memoirs, and was due to meet the archivist quite soon.

'Do you have any photos or programmes to send me, or have you written it up yourself?' she asked. I replied that I had no such plans. It had not been a happy time for me, and it was Susan herself who had stood by me, when I was "up agin" the management.

'I don't think Glyndebourne would want to hear MY recollections.'

'Of course they would,' replied Susan. 'Louise, that was over fifty years ago. They would be highly amused.'

As we talked and remembered the events, I began to think that it might, in fact, make a good story. We finished up by promising to swap reminiscences, and I was able to send her some good photographs of *She Stoops To Conquer*, a lovely period play in which we both took part.

The Children's Theatre was mainly educational. It aimed to bring the best plays, professionally acted, to the schools. We had signed quite a novel type of contract. We would be playing in London schools and halls for six weeks, and then touring outside London for another six weeks. Our producer wanted all of us to switch parts with each other for the second half of our contract period. He held the view that it would "freshen up the show". I was delighted with this arrangement, as I usually played character parts, and this would be my first ever opportunity to play the juvenile lead. So I worked hard learning the lines, understudying Merula Salaman (with whom I would be swapping parts) and working some of her moves into my own performance. She was Alec Guinness's wife.

All went well for the first three weeks. One afternoon, as I was making up after donning my *décolté* period costume, I felt my skin to be bumpy and irritable. When I looked more closely in the mirror, I discovered a bright red rash spreading rapidly from my chest up to my face. I felt terrible. It turned out to be measles. I was hustled home to my tiny bed-sitter in Earls Court, and the doctor was called. There was a restaurant in the basement of the building which could provide meals. The doctor warned me not to tell them that I had measles, as they would have been obliged to send me to a fever hospital. I was instructed to stay in bed until he called again.

There then ensued the loneliest week I have ever endured. The Children's Theatre crowd were too far away, and I knew no-one else to visit me. My current boy-friend was also on tour. He did manage one visit - if you could call it a visit - during which he wouldn't come through the door. He claimed never to have had measles, and didn't want to take the risk of catching them from me. He simply shoved in some books, some sucky sweets for my throat, murmured 'Take care, *my love*' from the safety of the landing outside the door, and departed! Yes indeed, my love! He plummeted in my estimation. My spirits plummeted in sympathy. I have never felt so low in my life - before or since - and it didn't help when even the doctor forgot to come on the day promised! (Needless to say, he remembered to send the bill on time.)

I despaired of ever getting going again, but then the weather took a hand. It was the spring of 1947 when an unusual amount of snow fell. During the end of my week in bed most of the country was paralysed. Susan had been my understudy, but she only got the chance to play my part of "Constance" for two days before the whole country had to be shut down, including all theatres. I was able to rejoin the company when they started up again. All then went smoothly. At the end of the first tour, there was to be a short break, followed by just one full rehearsal to get us going in our new parts. I went home to Ireland for a few days.

Almost as soon as I got there I received a telegram. It informed me that Merula was leaving us. It also asked me if I would mind playing my old part of "Constance", as they had taken on another actress to play "Kate". Of course, this was the leading part they had originally offered to me.

I phoned back to say that I did mind, and that I expected them to stick to their signed contract. 'Oh! but ...,' said the producer. 'We are having an extra rehearsal tomorrow ...'

'I'll be there,' I replied, and I was too.

I travelled overnight by ferry and the (by now familiar) long train journey to London. I never slept a wink. I had just time for a quick coffee before rushing in to the rehearsal.

I wasn't at all popular, as most of the old cast didn't want this extra rehearsal. The only support that I got was from Susan, and from Michael Martin-Harvey, a charming senior member of the company. He said, 'Of course you must play the part of Kate, and show them how it should be done.' He even took the trouble to bring me various embellishments to add to my period costume, so that he would be seen to encourage me. I was very touched.

In contrast, Donald Eccles asked me to have a cup of coffee with him in order to point out that, in his opinion, I couldn't play "Kate" because of my Irish accent. I pointed out that foreigners chose to come to Dublin to study the best English accent, as opposed to Oxford to study the likes of his! I also pointed out that the producer had specifically asked me to emphasise my Irish accent for the part of "Constance", who was supposed to be an Irish maid-servant. To cap it all, I expounded, Goldsmith was an Irishman! In the end we all struggled through to an agreement. I would play "Kate" as planned, and the new actress (I've forgotten her name) would play my old part of "Constance".

It wasn't until the second or third week of the tour that Donald could bring himself to acknowledge that I could play "Kate" very well.

Near the end of the tour, my mother decided to come and see me in my leading role. I had told her I might never get another one! As the night approached, I became very nervous. I was afraid that my really terrible memory might fail me. I had had so little rehearsal for this part and could feel the management's resentment - or felt I could. It didn't help when, the day before my mother was due to come, one of the doors in the elaborate stage set got stuck, and I was forced to exit through the wrong door. It upset me, tugging at that door with my back to the audience, trying to think of a line to "fill the gap". I thought it was intentional, and later I threw a tantrum at the stage manager (my first ever - perhaps Leading Lady syndrome)! He said nothing, but his expression clearly labelled me as an Irish trouble-maker, and not even worth an apology. Thankfully, all the doors worked the following night, and I managed quite a reasonably good performance for my mother. But I felt it was unlikely that I would be offered another part by the Children's Theatre.

Sadly this turned out to be true. Nonetheless, I valued my time in the Children's Theatre which I enjoyed for the most part, and during which I learned many of life's hard lessons.

Susan stayed on with the company, and was given some nice parts in the plays that followed. I never forgot how she had supported me, and we kept in touch. Many years later she came to visit us in Ireland and brought a friend. We took them swimming in a very chilly sea but thankfully it didn't stop them getting engaged. In due course my husband and I attended their very posh wedding in London.

Another general publicity theatre photograph (1949).
This was taken by Patrick Carey, one of the
well-known Dublin theatre family.

The Man With The Bowler Hat

He was a little man, small but neat, with a furled umbrella and a bowler hat. He knocked at the front door of my London flat and asked to see my radio licence. He appeared to be ticking off my name from a long list he carried. I was able to tell him that I had paid my licence, but when he asked about my neighbours upstairs I told him that I didn't know, as they were away. Then Agnes Browne, who was sharing my flat at the time, came up to admit, very shamefacedly, that she hadn't got hers yet as she had only just got her portable radio. She promised to obtain a licence as soon as possible. She was full of guilt and kept on apologising. We were to realise later that we had supplied all the information that he required without even a flicker of suspicion!

A week or two later, I was taking part in a BBC radio broadcast - one of a series. When I arrived home in the evening, I found the garden door ajar as was my semi-basement door to the flat. I wasn't alarmed to start with - I frequently forgot to lock up - until I realised that the door into the house above was also open. I had the key to this as my landlady and her husband - who were both in the theatre - were away. They had asked me to feed their cat as well as my own. I went straight up to see if they had come home unexpectedly. They weren't there and I continued up three flights of stairs to the top rooms. There I found my landlady's stage jewellry thrown all over the place - a terrible mess - and at last I realised there had been a burglary.

I suddenly felt very much alone up there. I was standing at the head of the stairs with my cat beside me - she had followed me all the way up. Now their cat appeared, just one flight below us. My jealous cat gave an unearthly screech and shot down the stairs to land on top of her. She reciprocated with an even worse scream of rage. I got such a fright that I nearly landed on top of both of them, but somehow I managed to get down the stairs again without getting scratched or bitten. I took a look into each room as I passed, and found to my surprise that the burglar - or burglars - hadn't disturbed any of them except to take the radio, plus the two from my flat. I was still shaking with fright as I phoned the police and, thankfully, they came around very quickly.

They were very supportive and kind, and helped me to put on the kettle for a comforting cup of tea. Then I explained that I was broadcasting in a weekly series, and would have to be out at precisely the same time the following week. I requested them to keep an eye on the house. They replied that they couldn't. They informed me that there was a break-in occurring in London, on average, every four minutes! They had only barely enough staff to get around the actual burglaries each day. They suggested that I ask a friend to sit in for me if I was still worried. They also told me that I had been very foolish to go upstairs before ringing them, as the burglars could have been there still, and would think nothing of knocking me on the head! I could feel the fear returning now and asked whether the burglar might come back later that night, but they thought not.

On their way out, they placed a number of small stones on top of the garden door, and said, 'If you hear the sound of even one stone dropping, phone us immediately - BEFORE you go out to look!'

Their actions and kind words were reassuring and, after adding a drop of whiskey to my hot "cuppa", I got myself off to bed. Agnes was away on tour so I was all alone, but, to my surprise, I got a good night's sleep. I found out later that the man who had visited us, supposedly to check our radio licences, must have been one of the gang.

Sure enough, the licensing authority informed us that they never sent out "little men in bowler hats!"

Dancing Hands

"Hey Diddle-ee-Dee! An Actor's Life for Me!"

Pinocchio's song expressed my own sentiments perfectly, but it wasn't always possible to find good parts to act. That's when I got involved in puppets. My reasoning went thus: if other people didn't provide the plays for me to act in, then at least I could take my puppets out onto the nearest street corner, and act non-stop for as long as I liked!

I never did achieve this exactly, but the London County Council did give us a contract to perform our road safety plays in several London parks, and later on we blossomed forth on BBC television. This all came about through John Wright and his Marionette Theatre.

John was an extremely gifted and well established puppeteer with his own permanent Marionette Theatre in Hampstead, North London. He was, however, new to glove puppets such as those that appear in a *Punch And Judy* Show. When he was sent a very attractive script for a glove puppet play called *Hansel And Gretel*, he was intrigued and decided to add it to his repertoire with his wife Zöe and myself as the puppeteers. We were both "resting" actresses and we had been doing voices for John's marionettes.

I was fascinated by the idea, having a natural affinity for glove puppets. They had seemed to stimulate all my creative powers ever since I had seen Tilly Losch. She was a vaudeville artiste with "dancing hands" whom I had seen performing in London. It was the first show I ever saw in London. I still have a clear picture in my mind of the darkened stage and the white gloved hands "dancing" to music - perhaps butterflies one moment, birds another, then a flower or a prayer. You couldn't see her at all, just the beautiful

Hansel And Gretel, *John Wright's Glove Puppets (1950).*

movements of the white hands. I was only about nine or ten years old, maybe younger, but I never forgot her and was to use some of her ideas in *Hansel And Gretel.*

I described it all in our brochure which we distributed in early 1950: "This new and original entertainment for children combines the charm and freshness of glove puppets with all the magic of the miniature theatre, complete with changes of scenery, lighting and music." I remember the creative pleasure I took in putting it all together. But first of all Zöe and I went up to Hampstead to find the *Punch And Judy* show that usually performed there. After watching it, we went behind and had a chat with the *Punch And Judy* man who was anything but encouraging. He took one look at two rather small females, and said 'You'll never do it Ma'am, it's far too much for a woman!' Maybe we should have listened to him, as it was only later on that we discovered how physically demanding it was.

But we weren't to be stopped, and next all three of us were off to Paris, where there was a long established glove puppet show in the Jardin de Luxembourg. There we watched quite an elderly puppeteer single handedly put on a wonderful children's show several times a day. He was most helpful and we were allowed to go behind the scenes to see how it was all done. We came back to London full of enthusiasm. Straight away, John got down to making some lovely puppets. The very talented lady who dressed John's marionettes made all the puppet costumes and props, while someone else constructed and painted scenery and assembled lighting and music. Zöe and I practised madly and tried to learn our lines, and soon - amazingly - we were in business!

Yes, we found it very hard work. With music and lighting also to contend with, we realised that we hadn't nearly enough hands and needed another puppeteer. We enlisted a keen supporter of ours, George Speaight, as a helper. We didn't realise that by doing so we became totally uneconomic. George was to say much later on that he should have told us to simplify the presentation rather than encouraging us to enlarge the company. But for the moment *Hansel And Gretel* was so successful that we failed to look ahead.

The trouble was that it only ran for 35 minutes and we soon found that we required a full hour's programme in order to get bookings away from home. At that time "home" was the Marionette Theatre, soon to be in full swing again showing *The Little Mermaid* - a great favourite. So *Hot-cockalorum* was developed for us to fill the gap. Then John, under tremendous pressure, managed to carve more puppets, and a beautiful soft puppet cat was made by the costume lady, using Minnie - my own cat - as a model. She had a black fluffy body and tail and a beautiful white shirtfront and paws, slanting green eyes, and many of Minnie's own mannerisms.

Then our tribulations began. First of all Zöe gave up and departed, having been offered work in the real theatre which she couldn't refuse, given that, at heart, she was an actress and not a puppeteer. Then we were asked to take part in a road safety awareness campaign organised by the London County Council. We were contracted to put on two shows a week in the Paddington Recreation Ground. The problem was that we found it very difficult to prepare the extra puppets and scenery in time. John was now busy again with his Marionettes, and possibly heartbroken at Zöe's departure. Things got more and more difficult, and finally I arranged with him to let me buy out the glove puppets and run them as my own company with the support of George Speaight.

Jack And The Beanstalk, *John Wright's Glove Puppets (1950).*

With hindsight, I know that this was a mistake and I was too impatient. John was an artist and couldn't be rushed or pushed, especially now his Zöe was gone. I never found anyone who could make puppets like him. This was made very clear later on, when the BBC would only accept John's work and turned down any other.

Just before we parted company with John Wright, in late 1950, a little white bear had been born in the London Zoo. He was named

Jeremy, the Giraffe, Hutton Puppet Theatre (1951).
Such a quiet, unassuming character - little did he know what complications life had in store for him!

"Brumas" - the first polar bear to be born in captivity - and he was a very popular character with the media and with all children. So we got a soft puppet called Brumas made for the road safety shows. He starred in a scene called *Brumas Learns The Highway Code*, and later on in our Christmas 1950 show called *Brumas Visits Father Christmas*. John had made us an intriguing Giraffe puppet before we split up. Later when we got a series of six Brumas plays on BBC television, "Giraffe" also became popular.

We had been introduced to a script writer called Milo Sperber who wrote the scripts for us and we did quite well up to the fifth performance. Milo always made his scripts a little too long for the time allotted to us and so far I had taken it for granted that I cut them down as required during rehearsal. But Milo objected before the fifth performance and wouldn't listen to reason. If the script required cutting, he was the person to cut it. When I didn't agree, he said he wouldn't write the sixth script and walked out on us!

There we seemed to be stuck, but I managed to write the sixth script myself, and we performed as usual thus completing the series. The BBC were quite unaware that it wasn't Milo's script! He, of course, was very angry and said he would sue us for using HIS Giraffe puppet and we had a stand-up fight at my flat. He claimed that the Giraffe's character was created by him and was thus copyright! All new ground to me. We had all planned the Giraffe together and had thrown in all our ideas when John was making the puppet, long before Milo had joined us. I had paid John for making him, so the puppet was clearly mine. Neither of us would give in, and Milo left in a temper. As he walked to the door, I felt I should call him back - quickly - but I didn't. I did nothing. I remember hearing a sound like a string breaking, and then he was gone.

I went to see the lady running the BBC *Children's Hour* programmes, to tell her about Milo and to ask about future dates. She referred it all to the BBC copyright department which eventually came back to us with their ruling. The puppet was indeed mine, but Milo could stop us if we so much as used one line previously written by him. I would have to change Giraffe's character completely! No easy task, as I was to find out when she sent me away to try and

Long before The Price Is Right, *Leslie Crowther helps out backstage for the Hutton Puppet Theatre (1952).*

write six more scripts without using a single line pre-empted by Milo. It took me six months of hardship, giving Giraffe an African voice and character, and what I thought were some lovely adventures suitable for a rod-puppet such as he. But all to no avail, as the *Children's Hour* programmer wouldn't accept them.

I felt very let down, and told her so, and fortunately she was very sympathetic and introduced me to a new script writer. She was Ruth Ainsworth who wrote the very popular *Listen With Mother* series. This always began with - 'Now, are you sitting comfortably? Then we'll begin ...'

Ruth came to see all my puppets and picked out the "Three Little Mushrooms". They had been created originally for *Hansel And Gretel*. The BBC never put on *Hansel And Gretel* in full - they thought the Witch was too frightening for the "very smalls". So Ruth, in her gentle calm way, comforted and calmed me and wrote six completely new scripts which were very suitable for the Little Mushrooms. The scripts were good, but there was no leading character such as Giraffe, and no real future in television for the time being.

Lob, Rush, Moon - The Three Little Mushrooms, *Hutton Puppet Theatre (1952). They appeared in their own weekly television show on the BBC.*

I knew it was my own fault. Once again, I had been impatient and tactless, and didn't listen to George who had been warning me to be careful. I should have waited until the series was over before having it out with Milo. He was probably afraid I was going to drop him. Maybe I would have too, as we didn't get on well together anyway. All George said was 'At least we know about copyright now!' Cold comfort to me, and now stress was beginning to take its toll. I developed a "spastic colon" which generated the worst pain I've ever known. The doctors just told me to look for another job.

So I headed back to Dublin in the spring of 1952, and a lovely spring it was too. I went riding with a farming friend of mine. The green fields were full of gambolling lambs and blossoming hedges, and I told her how much I wished I were a part of it.

'Well, why not,' said she. 'Now we've got tractors, and all the new machinery there's nothing to it. If I can farm so can you! Just buy a farm and get on with it!' And that set us all to thinking the impossible.

My mother and Bridie and Lizzie spent the summer searching for a small farm, while I went back to London to televise *The Three Little Mushrooms*. When I returned in the autumn, my mother met the Mail Boat in great excitement to tell me that they had found a farm!

I came off the boat on a Saturday. We travelled down to Ashford and inspected Ballinahinch Farm on Monday and I had it bought by Friday! I went back to London only to pack up my things and to cancel some Christmas bookings. When I told my two doctors that I was going to be a farmer, they laughed and said 'We think you have leaped out of the frying pan into the fire!'

And how right they turned out to be.

Ballinahinch

Ballinahinch Farm is situated on the Ashford-Roundwood road, about half a mile from Ashford village. Later on we would realise how lucky we were to be so near the village. It greatly enhanced the value of the place.

We were also lucky to have "Eileen's" just down at the corner, where our road joined the main road. "Eileen's" was the little shop which supplied us with all our necessaries, such as milk, bread and bananas - in fact, everything you could think of! It was run by Eileen Waters with Mary Gallagher's support. Although the shop itself was small, the house behind carried unknown quantities of "spares". We did most of our shopping there, and only once a week went as far as Wicklow Town.

But it wasn't the shopping that we valued most. Whenever we were looking for someone to do a job, such as gardening or cutting up firewood, we would go and ask Eileen if she knew anybody suitable. She usually did - Eileen knew everybody, and where they were and what there were doing at that moment. If Eileen recommended someone you knew that they would be all right, they wouldn't walk off with your valuables, and were probably good at the job as well. Even if we weren't looking for anyone, we got a great welcome and a good chat with all the news. With more shops like "Eileen's" no-one could ever feel lonely.

When we arrived in 1952, the farm consisted of nine small fields. We removed one internal hedge thus merging two fields into one, and in the late sixties we purchased another field from a neighbour. This later acquisition brought the acreage up to 72 statute acres, of which 69 are arable. Ballinahinch used to be an out-farm of the neighbouring Tottenham estate at Ballycurry. There remains to this day a very sturdy "famine wall" separating the two properties, which was commissioned by the Tottenham family to provide much-needed employment during the dreadful potato famines of the 1840s.

All the fields had been given individual names by the O'Reillys, and we retained most of these unchanged. In one of the fields close to the house there was an old lime kiln, which our predecessors had used to produce lime (for spreading on the fields). One of our first actions was to fill in this kiln, although the tell-tale "bump" remained to inspire us to invent an appropriate new name, i.e. Bumpy Field. The next field was Wood Field, occasionally into which I have seen the wild deer leap from the woods, clearing quite a high hedge. Then came Hollow Field, and Rectory Field leading down to the road. Homeward was through Chance Field, leading into The Paddock. Across the road there were another three fields.

As I write these words, The Paddock is full of wild daffodils. Looking at them, I am reminded of how lucky I have always been to live here.

Ballinahinch - our country farm (1953).

When my mother had started searching for a suitable property, she had enlisted the help of an old family friend called Colonel Chapman - or just "The Colonel", as we called him. She believed that he knew all about farming. Actually we found out later that he didn't. He just wanted to get rid of some old farm machinery he had

Ballinahinch yard (1953). It remains mostly unchanged nearly fifty years later, although in 1980 we converted the outhouses at the far end into a small cottage.

on his hands! But I have to give him the credit for doing the bargaining for me, and actually managing to beat down the price by quite a considerable amount - something I would never have been able to do by myself.

You would think that I could remember what I paid for my first and only farm - but I cannot. I do remember that we signed the deeds in October 1952, and paid the purchase price in installments over the next two months. I have discovered a record of the final payment of £3,412 10s 0d which was made on December 20, 1952. That probably means that the total price was less than £5,000. As it happened, we were lucky to have chosen a period during which land prices were at their lowest for a generation. Just another example of the good fortune which has stood by me for most of my life.

The O'Reillys moved out in January 1953, and Bridie and I moved in. There was such a lot to contend with before my mother could join us. The house had to be altered quite a bit, and Bridie and I hoped to paint the inside ourselves. The builders we had in were constructing the new wing or "granny flat" in which my mother would be living. Mr. Butler, of Dawson Street, was our architect, and he designed a six-room extension which included a living room, two bedrooms, two bathrooms and a toilet. Before that, our toilet facilities consisted of a small shed outside in the yard. The extension almost doubled the size of the house, although it made it very long.

My mother came down quite often bringing her very efficient gardener, Bob. Not only did he make the garden, levelling a lot of it by hand (no JCBs in those days), but he often helped us with other jobs. My mother had found me in tears on one of her visits, because as fast as I painted the pantry walls the plaster fell down and I hadn't a clue what to do about it! Now I know that I should have replastered the whole pantry before painting, rather than trying to patch it and paint over the patches. There was only a fortnight left before my mother was due to move in. So Bob was summoned in from the garden to finish the pantry, and after this he found himself on the top of a ladder painting the high ceiling in the dining room!

My mother took over the new "living room", turning it into a small, self-contained apartment with her own furniture. She also had a separate bedroom in the old part of the house. I settled into the large bedroom at the end of our new home, although as time would tell I wouldn't stay there for long.

The Sound Of Running Water

The sound of running water calms
        And soothes the busy brain.
I love to stand and listen to
        My stream soon after rain.

It chuckles as it trickles over
        Every tiny fall,
Then flows on to the river -
        It seems past all recall.

When the river joins the ocean
        Merging in immensity,
My stream is lost, but maybe finds
        A sparkling new identity.

Becomes white-crested rhythmic waves
        That break upon the shore,
Or joins the clouds that bring the rains
        To thirsty lands once more.

Or born aloft by fleecy clouds
        That sail across the blue,
It falls at last on Wicklow hills
        And joins my stream anew.

From heathery source to my green fields
        Between familiar banks,
Where flowers abound, and birds and trees,
        And I still stand entranced.

When my turn comes, I wonder -
        As I listen to your voice -
When my small stream of being joins
        The sea ....
        Will I still have a choice?

The Wedlocks

After I bought the farm, we couldn't move in straight away as I didn't gain possession for three months. This was to allow the O'Reillys time to take out their root crops, and also to find a new house to move into. I gathered that it wouldn't be in the countryside. The O'Reillys wanted out of farming. In fact, Mrs. O'Reilly dreamed of having a little shop and was planning to move nearer town.

During the interval we were allowed to start farming the rest of the land. As soon as I got back from winding up things in London, Bridie and I started coming down from Foxrock every day to do whatever we could. Apart from a couple of stubble fields, and the aforementioned root crops, the rest of the farm was in grass. We were advised to "set it" for six months as we had no animals of our own to put on it. We were lucky to find the Wedlocks to take it. They were three brothers who farmed up near Roundwood, said to be the highest village in Ireland, where it was much colder and the grass was scarce. We were told that they were "great characters" but very reliable, which thankfully turned out to be true.

On the day they were due to arrive, in January 1953, it was a sunny, mild day. Bridie and I made a special effort to get to Ballinahinch early to be ready to receive them. We thought they would bring the cattle in the morning, but the morning came and went and nobody appeared. The afternoon passed slowly as we waited expectantly. After a long while, we began to think they weren't coming at all, as it was getting "dusky".

We were on the point of departure when we heard their loud, cheerful voices preceding them down the road. I had just enough time to station Bridie on the road below our gate when in they came, filling the yard with turmoil and sound as they shouted at the excited animals amid their greetings to us.

'How are ye ma'am? Are ye keepin' well?' followed by 'Git on dere - dat's the gate over dere, isn't it Michael?' to Mr. O'Reilly, who had come out to help.

There were three of them and they seemed larger than life, with big hearty voices. They each had a sack of cattlefood over one shoulder. We mere city folk dubbed them "The Mountainy Men", which title stuck in our heads through all our dealings with them.

'I'm sure ye thought we was never comin',' said Billy, whom I took to be the eldest. 'But the grass up above has been gone this long time and we let dem get a good feed on the way down!'

Afterwards we learned that he was referring to the "Long Acre", or the luxuriant grass and weeds growing all along the side of most Irish roads. I gathered that they had allowed the cattle to graze the verges, as they walked them the six or seven miles between the farms, taking most of the day to do it! In those days, there was very little traffic on the back roads, and the Wedlocks were not the men to miss out on such a bonanza.

We became very attached to the Wedlocks - Billy, John and Jim - and looked forward to their visits. They had three sisters, but the girls had all left home to get married, or to get a job, and the boys looked after themselves. Still in their thirties and quite good looking, it was surprising they never got married themselves, being so friendly and always cheerful. At the start, they brought extra food for the cattle, but as the grass got plentiful it was extra animals they brought. They would buy these in the Sales Yard down in Ashford, if they got the chance and the price was right.

We were really sorry to see them go after the six months were up, as they had been so helpful. However Bridie and I often met them at the sales yard, and the moment they saw us they would rush over to chat being genuinely interested in how we were getting on.

'How are ye doing up dere, Ma'am?' they would ask, and they were always ready to give us a hand if we needed it.

Kids' Play

I had been offered a nanny goat by some of my Foxrock friends and we were delighted with the idea, little knowing what we were letting ourselves in for. I was only worried about how she should be transported from Dublin. In the end, we took out the back seat of my elderly Morris Minor, and Nanny - as we named her, rather unimaginatively - fitted perfectly into the resulting hollow. She seemed to enjoy the ride.

Nanny loved the plentiful fresh grass in the paddock, and settled in as though she had lived there for ever. However, a big surprise lay in store for us. It was only about two weeks after her arrival that Bridie came rushing in to find me, saying 'Ma'am, ye'll never guess - Nanny's got twins!'

'You mean she's produced kids?'

'Yes Ma'am, and they're lovely. When I opened the door this mornin' there they were, drinkin' their mammy's milk. I'll be able to milk her, Ma'am, when I get a milk can.' Bridie was very excited. 'Maybe I'll get the loan of a jug from Mrs. O'Reilly!'

It happened to be Good Friday, so inevitably the kids were named Goody and Friday. Nanny had such a thick shaggy coat that we had never noticed her condition - shows you how much we knew about goats! The kids were adorable, and Nanny produced such a quantity of lovely milk that there was plenty for them and the house as well. I became addicted to goat's milk - it has much more flavour than cow's milk.

Nanny had her own form of addiction, however, which was to eat her way through any hedge with which she came in contact, and particularly that one which belonged to our neighbour, Mrs. King-Gill. She was a keen gardener and she had many beautiful plants and shrubs in her garden. Unfortunately, Nanny loved them too! We fenced and fenced again, but she always managed to find a new way of getting in.

We got used to Mrs. King-Gill arriving on our doorstep in high dudgeon! Bridie began to know by the expression on her face as she strode up the road, that Nanny had eaten her way through again. As a result, she - Bridie - would hide and leave it to me to do my best to apologise, and offer to replace the vandalised shrubs. To do Mrs. King-Gill justice, she never took me up on my various offers. Perhaps she was doubtful about our gardening skills, but I think she just wanted the opportunity to "give off" and to flatten me! I had disrupted her a lot when I first arrived. I had had no telephone to start with, and had to ask to use hers for a whole six months before I managed to get one of my own. Relations became strained to say the least!

Nanny, Goody and Friday in Ballinahinch yard (1953). You have to look closely to spot the second kid.

Hedges have always been a problem at Ballinahinch as there are so many of them. We didn't have Wat (Walter Carroll) with us at that stage, who later on would keep things in order. The Ashford to Roundwood road runs right through the farm, cutting it in half with long hedges on both sides. Wat, being a County Council roadworker, was often on this part of the road and had been given numerous cups of tea by Lizzie and Bridie. In due course, when he retired, he had no real home to go to and Bridie and Lizzie welcomed him as a friend. Soon he started doing odd jobs for them around the house and yard, and gradually took over all the hedges. Wat loved working on his own, and if we were looking for him we would probably find him weeding away contentedly in the shrubbery, down the back end of the garden. Eventually, Bridie asked my mother if Wat could move into the attic room over the kitchen, and he became a familiar member of the growing "community" at Ballinahinch.

Meanwhile the kids were growing, and they found out that it was great *craic* to play on the heaps of sand which had been stacked up in the yard by the builders. Nobody seemed to notice what a mess they were making. Then came the disastrous day when they discovered that they could jump from a particular pile, which was stacked against the wall, and up onto the roof of the range of outhouses which ran right along the other side of the yard. This included the cow house, barn, stable, henhouse, etc.. They had great fun chasing each other from one end to the other, clattering over the old pink tiles, and cracking many of them en route. We were able to flatten that particular heap of sand, but we knew that sooner or later they would find some other form of "divilment". They had already shown they took after their mother with regard to hedges and tasty garden flowers! So it was with great reluctance that I decided the goats must GO, as we couldn't cope with them.

I realised that it was no wonder our Foxrock friends had been glad to find Nanny a happy home with me. Now I was pleased to remember that they had promised to take her back if she turned out to be troublesome. So I was able to give her a return trip in the faithful Morris Minor. I heaved a great sigh of relief when I said 'Goodbye', and drove away feeling as a convict must feel on his first day out of prison.

We still had to get rid of the kids, now old enough to give the unwary a heavy "bunt", if only in play. Goody was easy, as lots of people like goats milk, but it took us quite a long time to find a happy home for Friday. It's well known that putting a goat to graze with cattle is a good idea, as the goat will eat the weeds which don't suit the cattle. Eventually he did join such a herd, but not before he was a year old, and we heaved another collective sigh of relief!

In a way, we were also sad. We loved our goats, and Nanny would always be remembered as our first farm animal and the first to have young.

Warmth

What are we looking for now we are old?

It's warmth I am looking for now I am old
Warmth of body and warmth of mind
My open fire's a joy to me
With the dog at my feet and the cat on my knee
But I like to stay watching

The action I find
Is with youth
Is with heat
For the heat will bring anger
And anger is needed
To stir them to action
To my satisfaction
Especially if my opinions are heeded
But just warmth is enough for me
Now I am old

Cows

Bridie and I were never in doubt as to what mode of farming we wanted to pursue. We wanted to be in milk and I wanted Kerry cows. I reckoned the Kerries were the only milking cows which were both exclusively Irish and which could rival the Jerseys.

To start with we couldn't find Kerries locally and I compromised by buying two Jerseys from a well known herd nearby. They were guaranteed to be in calf, but one of them - Carita - never came in calf at all in that first season. I wrote several letters claiming compensation for the loss of a year, without success. When she eventually did have a calf it was small and delicate and never did well. One day, it fell ill and died just as the vet drove into the yard. I remember the moment so vividly. We were in the calfhouse when we heard his car drive in, then the calf bellowed, rolled over in the straw with all four legs in the air, and died!

It was a comical affair when we eventually got around to putting Carita into calf. There was a Jersey bull nearby at Ballyhenry, and we made an appointment with Mrs. Richards, his owner, for Carita to be serviced. Seamus Kavanagh, my tractor man, took the little cow in the trailer, and I went along in my car. I was all prepared to watch the deed, dressed for action even down to very mucky gumboots.

However, on my arrival I was informed that Mrs. Richards was expecting me in the drawingroom. There she informed me very firmly that 'Ladies never watch these performances,' and I found myself sitting at a lace covered table complete with the best tea service, hot scones and polite conversation. I felt frustrated but amused, and at the same time developed a great admiration for my hostess. Later on we became great friends. I was often invited to tea, which she poured from the heavy silver teapot with an increasingly shakey hand (due to the onset of Parkinson's Disease).

My second Jersey cow had the extraordinary name of "Maiden-Sin". She did calve when expected, but it was a bull-calf and her milk yield wasn't all that great. I was so busy trying to claim for Carita that I never got the opportunity to find out why she was called "Maiden-Sin". Was it High Church, anti-sex mentality or was it a celebration? She was certainly very beautiful with her pale gold colouring and big, dark brown eyes.

Bridie didn't really mind what breed we had just so long as she had cows to care for. She loved milking them and was never happier than when her head was pressed hard against a warm flank, hearing the "phut phut" of the milk spurting into the pail. She would talk to them and sing to them, even bringing my tape recorder out into the cowhouse, as she said music made them give more milk. We noticed that one of the Wedlocks - Jim I think it was - was often in the cowhouse at milking time. He said he liked to hear the music, but we wondered if it was the opportunity to have a good long chat with Bridie that drew him! So in a way - I suppose rather selfishly - I was a bit relieved, when the Wedlocks left us, that no romance had developed for Bridie. Farming at Ballinahinch could hardly have continued if she had departed in order to run the Wedlock farm!

After Nanny had returned to Foxrock, and whilst we were waiting for the Jerseys to come into calf, we needed to come by some milk for the household. We were advised to ask a certain John Tyner to help us to find a cow which was already in milk. He very kindly took us to the Ashford sales mart and helped us to buy, quite inexpensively, a rather ordinary little cross-bred cow. She turned out to be a marvellous milker. After this we regarded John (my future husband) as an expert in the buying of cows. On another occasion when we found him to be at an auction where we hoped to buy more cows, we had no qualms about standing behind him. If we saw him bid for an animal, we would bid for it too as we knew it would be a good one! Reprehensible behaviour, of course, and I never owned up to it. No doubt if I had he would have seen the funny side, and taken it as a compliment.

At last there came the day when four Kerry heifers were advertised for sale in our local paper. I arranged by telephone to go and see them at a farm somewhere down in County Carlow. I went in my Morris Minor and Seamus followed with our tractor and a trailer which, needless to say, I had borrowed from John. We liked the look of the heifers, and we loaded all four of them into the trailer and set off for home.

All went well until we got to the Shillelagh side of Tullow where a downpour of rain hit us. It was real cloudburst stuff and Seamus dropped behind. I went back to find him and he had drawn into the side of the road, under the trees, for shelter. There were no cabs on the tractors in those days and he was literally soaked to the skin. I told him to take my car and drive home fast, get changed into some dry clothes and come straight back to relieve me. In the meanwhile I would be driving the tractor at my own slow pace.

To start with I wasn't doing badly as the rain had stopped and the road was flat. But two or three miles outside Shillelagh, just before Ballyrahan House, there is a long winding hill. On this fateful day it had been made very slippery with flood water still streaming down the middle. I took it too slowly and about halfway up I knew I would have to change gear. Not having driven a tractor for quite a while, much less with a trailer loaded with animals, I made a mess of it and suddenly lost speed. This made the cattle shift in the trailer which subsequently tilted backwards. This in turn lifted the tractor wheels off the road so that they couldn't get any purchase on the water-washed surface. Then, to my horror, the whole contraption started to slide backwards down the hill!

It was the first time I had ever felt all the hairs on my head, and all the non-existent ones on my spine, to stand up for at least two minutes as we slid right down to the bottom of the hill. It gave me plenty of time to wonder what would happen. Would we turn over into the ditch? Was this the end of me? To my surprise we slid to a standstill quite safely and I was able to breathe again! We were just lucky that nobody else had followed us up the hill. Now we were blocking the road, so eventually I managed to manoeuvre a bit and straighten up the trailer. Then the cattle regained their usual position, and, in bottom gear, I took a run at the hill and got to the top successfully at long last. But my confidence was very shaken. I became more and more anxious as I realised that Rathdrum was still to come, with its long, narrow, twisting road down to the river and then the steep, turning hill up the other side. I wondered whether I should attempt it at all, although that I knew the cattle would get restive if I stopped for long.

Fortunately, Seamus got back to rescue me before I reached Rathdrum and I handed over to him with great relief. We all got home safely that night, but I decided that driving a tractor pulling a trailer loaded with live cattle was one thing I would not be doing again!

Old Bones

I feel depressed, my spirits are low,
I've a meeting tonight, but my old bones say 'No!
The wind has turned bitter - we don't want to go.'
But I know ...
There's a new chairperson - committee's new too,
They need my support - there's so much to do.
Then the phone speaks:
'We don't have the room - it's postponed for two weeks.'
My old bones rattle and dance with glee
And say 'Now you're not driving - so whiskey in tea!'
After which my dog and I climb our green hill,
And I stand there well warmed and gazing my fill
As the evening sun spotlights the landscape to show
My incredible wealth in silver and gold.
No wonder the sun was worshipped of old.
Now it shines through a hole in the dark April clouds
And highlights the deep gold of fragrant gorse
Which frames a green field with a grazing white horse,
Studded with ewes and their lambs newborn
Near the silvery haze of spikey blackthorn
All mingling with palest green pussey-willow
Seeming soft enough to stuff my pillow.
Next to be lit are my two damson trees
All decked with blossom and busy with bees,
Framing newly sown curving potato drills
Which bring in the gold to pay all the bills.
Now in the paddock full of gold daffodils
Then shining afar lighting blueblack hills

Before coming back to the bank of my stream
Where the primroses catch the wandering beam.
Even the tiny fresh leaves of the May
Show up so clearly tho' quite far away.
Now the sun's gone 'twill be chilly quite soon
And the birds are singing their drowsiest tune.
So I turn and see rising an apricot moon!
Huge and surprising - it's not even dark
But maybe I'm viewing the next Noah's Ark!
It's clear that the sun has a message for me -
'If we squander the beauty of all that we see
We may bring to the moon Irish whiskey in tea!'

Susannah

Susannah was a revelation to me. I had all a "townie's" preconceptions about pigs in general, and was quite sure they were dirty, smelly, obstinate creatures, reportedly difficult to manage. But Bridie, who loved pigs with passion, persuaded me to try them out.

'Give a pig a proper house and clean beddin' and they're lovely animals,' said she, 'and twice as intelligent as anythin' else.'

This we were to find out from Susannah, who was indeed most elegant, from the tips of her neat little cloven hooves to her curly tail. She had firm, pink curves and surprisingly intelligent eyes in a face full of character. We had chosen her with care, from a beautiful herd of gilts belonging to Colonel Adams of Newtownmountkennedy, partly because of her well bred looks but also because she was due to have a family in about a fortnight. Bridie considered that this would be long enough for her to settle down, and for us to finish off the house we had been preparing for her. But Susannah, possibly a bit shaken after being transported by lorry, had different ideas. I can see her now as she minced delicately down the narrow gangplank as if walking a tightrope. She immediately started to "make her bed" which, of course, meant that she was getting down to business just as soon as she could collect some straw into one corner!

We had planned "a creep" with a heat lamp in the next corner, so that the little piglets would be warm but safe from their mother, who could otherwise accidentally roll over and squash them. The concept was that they could get to and from her, but the bottom bar was positioned too low to allow her to follow. The trouble was that we had counted upon having the fortnight to put the creep in place, and we hadn't finished erecting it. Here was Susannah already beginning to have her family! Two or three of the tiny newborn piglets were lying snug, under the lamp, before there was a pause long enough to put the prepared barrier across the corner. I was left holding it temporarily in place, whilst Bridie and Pat (Kavanagh) went off to fetch some concrete blocks from the haggard with which to secure it.

Susannah chose this particular moment to find out where her newborn piglets had gone. I thought that I would be safe on the far side of the barrier, but Susannah rose on her hind legs and scared the wits out of me, as she was then tall enough to reach me over the top. I had been warned several times about the strength of her jaws, and how she could bite through an arm with the greatest of ease. I began to shout for help, evading her as best I could by shifting from one end of the planking to the other. I just managed to hold out long enough (as poor Susannah was overtaken by more birth-pangs) to escape, and finally the blocks were put into place as even more little pigs arrived. To our delight, she was to have eleven of them in all.

It was now dark and windy and cold. We had given Pat his tea earlier on, so that he could stay watching over Susannah, replacing the little piglets under the lamp whenever they ceased to feed. It was fascinating to see how they were able to crawl over their Mum, or under each other, until they found a spare teat, and then could fasten on until they were satisfied. They often fell asleep still attached. The main danger at this point was that Susannah would turn over and suffocate them all unintentionally. I went out later with a hot mug of tea for Pat, and found him still sitting on a stool close by the sow. He expected that there would be more little arrivals. He was in such a draught that I thought I would shut the half-door, and was slipping in the bolt on my side when there was an agonised shout from Pat:

'Jaysus, Mrs! Will ye leave the bloody door open on me! D'ye want her to ate me alive?!'

I unshot the bolt and left him to freeze, but brought him out an extra coat!

Such are the tribulations of pig farmers, and thanks to Pat's care we had no losses on this our first attempt. It is usual to allow the sow three months or so feeding the bonhams, or "bons", until they can forage for themselves, or until her milk begins to dry up. Then she can be put in pig again. In Susannah's case, this, of course, entailed a return visit to Colonel Adams' piggery and the boar.

I had had a crate made for the journey which could be bolted onto the box, or carrier behind the tractor, but I hadn't thought it necessary to put a roof on it. Once again, I misjudged Susannah's height when standing on her hindlegs. When Pat reached the village, she managed to hop out onto the road opposite the Catholic church. The door happened to be open and in Susannah went! It was fortunate that there was no service taking place, as she was halfway up the centre aisle before they managed to get ahead of her and stop her!

Since then, I have often wondered if it was just an effort on her part to escape an undignified mode of transport, or if it was sheer curiosity. Perhaps she wanted to say her prayers before she went "coortin'"! I'm told that Pat only managed to get her back into the crate with the help of Father Meehan, the parish priest. He seemed to understand pigs and had a knack of dealing with Susannah. He even produced some strong cord with which to tether her for the onward journey. Anyway, all went to plan thereafter. I had a top made for the crate to be used on the next trip - if any.

Susannah and her family in the orchard (1953).

To add to our general discomfiture the "bons" were acting up as well. They were allowed out by day into the little orchard to forage for themselves. What we didn't know was that they had found a way up into Bumpy Field, just above the orchard, where our milking cows were grazing. We had been puzzled for some time that the milk yield of one of our best young newly calved cows, called Rosie, had suddenly gone down. She seemed quite healthy. The mystery was only explained when, just by chance, Bridie caught the eleven little pigs drinking on tiptoe from Rosie's well-filled udder.

They probably regarded her as their private milk-bar! No wonder they did so well, and sold so well when their time came! Rosie enjoyed it too. She probably missed her calf!

By this time we had our doubts as to the profitability of such a small venture. We decided to keep a careful account of all costs, from the moment Susannah was put into pig to the moment her family was sold as bonhams. We were to be shocked later on, when all was totted up, that the only profit for us was "the runt". This was the smallest of the little pigs and was sold eventually for just £3! This didn't include anything for all the work we'd put into Susannah and her progeny. It was indeed a labour of love, and we learned that, to make a profit, pigs had to be kept on a much larger scale.

Little angels, surely - but only because they are sleeping (1954).

So, very regretfully, we decided to cut our losses and sell poor Susannah as soon as she had finished feeding her next batch of "bons". We weren't looking forward to that time as we had grown very attached to her and the little piglets, but we couldn't afford a loss-making set-up. Into the bargain, she was certainly a bit of a handful on occasion, as we were yet to find out.

I thought I might be able to cut down on expensive pigfood by letting her out in daytime to forage for herself. I had read about a harness for pigs attached to a long chain. We planned to bolt this to the inside of quite a spacious, moveable wooden chicken house -

with nests and perches removed, of course - which we had picked up at an auction. The whole contraption could then be moved onto fresh grass whenever necessary, and there was plenty of that in the paddock. This would stop Susannah from roaming through our neighbours' gardens, or through our farm crops.

She seemed to take to this very happily ... but first impressions can be deceiving.

One morning, Bridie came hurrying in to me with a very long face.

'Oh! Ma'am, come quickly! Something terrible's after happenin' to Susannah - she's passed right out!'

I hurried out, and found that Susannah had pulled all the straw out of her house and was lying under the heap, all stiff and cold. She did indeed look dead, but I found she was still breathing faintly. I tried to rub and slap some warmth into her, while Bridie ran to get some hot food to offer her. All to no avail - she paid us not the slightest attention.

I sent Bridie off to get more help to move her, and meanwhile undid the straps of her harness and was trying to get it off her. At that instant, Susannah suddenly came back to life, leapt to her feet, snorted vehemently and made off at top speed! She wouldn't let us catch her for ages, cantering away as soon as we got near before snorting again. We reckoned she was laughing at us! Finally, to our great relief, she consented to come in to her proper house for her evening meal.

Do you think she planned it all, or did she just get tired of the smell of chickens and decide to sleep out? Then again, perhaps she got cold and pulled the straw over her to keep herself warm? Did this resuscitate her? I'm afraid we'll never know.

We found her a good home when the time for parting came - but we made certain that it was too far away to keep in touch!

Fodder Beet

By far the worst disaster to hit Ballinahinch occurred in 1954 - the year we grew the fodder beet.

We now had eight milking cows to feed. They were put out on grass during the day, but the concentrated foodstuff which we gave them at each milking was very expensive. We thought that the fodder beet would provide a good, cost-effective replacement. The milking cows were all tied up at night, each in her separate stall in the cowhouse. This happened to be just opposite my bedroom window. I was never an early riser, so Bridie liked to bring me my breakfast in bed, and then she was free to go out and milk the cows, and feed them before letting them out.

On this particular day, it must have been in early May, I was sitting up in bed with my tray on my knee, when I saw Bridie running out of the cowhouse looking very distressed. She was soon telling me 'Ma'am, all the cows are down in their chains and can't get up! Oh Ma'am, it's terrible!'

I got out there very quickly, took one look and rang the vet who was able to come immediately. He diagnosed it as fodder beet poisoning just as soon as he knew that we had a field of it. What we didn't know when we grew it was that although the root - which is like that of sugar beet - is splendid feeding when harvested, the green tops are highly poisonous, alive or dead. The cows had been grazing across the road in "Four Acres", and had broken into the fodder beet next door through a gap in the fence.

Poor Bridie was devastated. She regarded each of the cows as a personal friend and knew them all by name. They were in obvious pain and distress. The vet worked very hard, and as a result of injections and repeated douches five of them were back on their feet again before nightfall. Another two made it the next day, but one never got up again. For the next fortnight, we made valiant efforts to keep her going, spreading thick straw under her, bringing her water in a bucket and what food she could manage to eat. Try as she might, even with the men helping to lift her, she never got further than her knees, and grew steadily weaker.

We were so sad in the end to have to put her down, but the vet agreed that we should save her from further suffering.

It seemed that we had to learn the hard way. Needless to say, we never grew fodder beet again.

The Tap

Every time I pass The Tap - which is a pleasant pub on the Wicklow-Arklow road - I am reminded of a previous happy occasion.

One day, I was driving along the road when I suddenly ran out of petrol. As it happened I stopped outside The Tap. I managed to pull in off the main road, and made my way inside. I was hoping that I could "beg, borrow or steal" enough fuel to get me to the next petrol station. Once inside I found that there was a wedding in full swing.

My heart sank, as I realised that the staff would be far too busy to cope with silly people needing petrol, and everybody else was very pre-occupied with having a good time. Nonetheless, I got a great welcome from one young man who was impeccably dressed in wedding garb - tails, a shining white shirt, carnation buttonhole - and who wielded a large bottle of champagne. He introduced himself as Gerry and asked me to go dancing with him.

I managed to deflect him long enough to focus on my need for petrol. We were assisted by another wedding guest, called Pádraig, who offered to see if the car would run on champagne.

'Oh no,' said Gerry. 'Champagne's made for drinking ...'

'Good idea,' said Pádraig, disappearing into the depths of the pub. He returned with a bottle of his own, and soon I found myself sitting at a table drinking champagne, while my two knight-errants discussed how to get petrol from their car into mine.

'It's easy,' said Gerry, 'just suck it out!'

'It's much nicer to suck champagne,' retorted Pádraig. 'What kind of a car have you got?'

'It's a Renault,' I said.

'There y'are!' exclaimed Pádraig. 'It's French. Sure all French drivers use champagne!'

'Only when they win a race,' said Gerry, very sensibly.

'No! No!' retorted Pádraig, as he swung gently from side to side and came close to spraying us. 'You haven't won a race yet ...'

He then disappeared for a second time, only to return with the kindly barman, who seemed to be called Liam. Liam located a rubber tube from somewhere which would enable us to siphon out some petrol from their car into mine. We were on our way outside when they realised that they must have something into which to put the petrol.

'If only we could get hold of an empty bottle ...' I began before I could stop myself.

They both agreed that they must empty their bottles, and the thoughtful Liam provided a plate of delicious sandwiches to eat with the wine. By this time I was enjoying myself far too much to worry.

'Imagine,' I said to myself, 'here I am with two gorgeous young men looking after me, which doesn't happen very often!' Enjoy to the full the present moment - that's what all the philosophers tell us.

In the end I was quite sorry when they managed, perhaps with a little help from Liam, to transfer some petrol into my car. They couldn't remember where they had parked their own car, so we chose the longest, most sumptuous-looking car that we could see. I hoped that the owner would never miss the two champagne bottles full of the precious liquid which got me started on my way home.

Did I say earlier - "beg, borrow or STEAL"?

Avoca

I have no reliable recipe for catching a husband - in fact quite the opposite. I kept on losing or escaping possibilities until I was over forty, and then found the right man in spite of myself, and the weather! With hindsight, I'm sure that laughter had as much to do with it as anything else.

Lizzie and Bridie agreed with this explanation up to a point. They were inveterate match-makers so long as it wasn't for themselves.

'A lovely man, Miss L, to make ye laugh,' said Lizzie.

Bridie agreed, but added 'What takes his fancy, Ma'am, is us knowing so little about cows an' all, that he has to come an' rescue us ....'

'Yis,' cut in Lizzie. 'Ye brought in the Kerries, Ma'am, without ever findin' out was there a Kerry bull near enough. Anyways yez have half his machinery borrowed ....' and she tailed off, perhaps feeling she had said enough.

Lizzie very often brought me down to earth. It was true that whenever I needed any particular implement I'd borrow it from John Tyner, and his story later was that he had to marry me to get them back! Fortunately there was a Kerry bull in County Wicklow, but only at the far end of the Vale of Avoca - a fair distance to go in a hurry. Of course, we had no artificial insemination in those days.

It was the early spring of 1954. For some reason which I can't remember now, we had missed out on getting Roisín into calf, and I was watching her anxiously determined not to miss her again. Well, she came into season all right, but it was right in the middle of a snowstorm! It kept us pinned down for days and we couldn't do anything about it. Finally it stopped and the sun came out and the snow began to melt around us, but the roads were still all hard-packed snow. I knew Roisín couldn't last much longer. I rang John to know whether we could go, and also could I borrow the trailer he had promised to lend us? He said 'Yes, but take care on those roads.'

Seamus went down to Cronykeery to fetch the trailer, whilst I phoned the people in Avoca. They thought the roads would be alright for a tractor, but warned me not to bring my car down their lane. So off we went and got there safely in three hours or so.

On our arrival, the tractor managed the lane without difficulty. It was slightly downhill with a sort of dip halfway. Roisín went off to meet her bull. I went off shopping in the meanwhile, and came back later when it was time to bring her home. All had gone well, but now the sun had gone down and the frost was taking over again. Seamus was going uphill this time and he got stuck in the hollow. Nothing we could do would get him out again, either forwards or backwards! The farmer tried to pull him out with his tractor and chain, but all the wheels just spun on the icy surface. It began to get very cold and our host said we couldn't leave Roisín in an open trailer any longer. He offered to put her up for the night. So we managed to unload her again, and a place was found for her in the stable between two big farm horses.

I have a wonderful picture of her in my mind, placidly eating some hay, lit by a lantern provided by our host, and watched by the two big horses, one on each side of her. They looked back at me every now and then as if to say - 'What have we done to deserve this?'

Seamus and I walked up the slippery lane, past the abandoned tractor and trailer, and I drove him home. I worried all the way back what I was going to say to John - well, partly worrying but at the same time glad of the opportunity to ask his help again! Thankfully, John just sounded amused and said he knew someone down there (I never knew him NOT to know someone locally) who would solve all our problems. He arranged to pick us up early next day, and I was able to go to bed comforted and looking forward to the morrow.

The morning appeared at last and the sky was blue, with the sun shining brightly on the remaining snow. John called for us early while the air was still "sparkley and tingley" and my spirits soared as he drove so carefully along the icy roads. John had phoned Tommy

Crammond, an old friend of his, who had a farm very nearly opposite the one where the trailer was stuck, and he was to meet us there shortly.

The fun began when John put a halter on Roisín and tried to lead her up the lane to where the trailer was parked. The hard frost during the night had turned the surface into slippery ice, and neither John's gumboots nor Roisín's neat little hooves could get any purchase on it. So when John pulled on the rope she came willingly enough, but then couldn't stop and he in his turn was pulled off his feet. When he got going again she was doing double "splits" and I was dying with laughter, as the two of them repeatedly pulled each other forward in short dashes. John caught the laughter when Roisín bellowed, and we all got more and more helpless, until Seamus came to our assistance and we finally got her back into the trailer.

By that time Tommy Crammond had arrived with a much bigger tractor and a longer chain. He pulled our tractor and trailer and Roisín up to the road with the greatest of ease. Soon afterwards Seamus set off for home.

John and I had been invited to stay for lunch by Sophie Crammond, who was a famous cook. She and Tommy had a family of eight - six girls and two boys - most of whom came out to meet us and pelt us with snowballs! Perhaps they were also checking me out! John told me much later on that they had been trying to get him married off again ever since his first wife had died. They had heard tell of his new girlfriend.

'GIRLFRIEND - did you say?'

'Well, you looked so happy that day after the snow-balling, that they took you to be younger than you actually were. There was a rumour going round that you were Betty Hutton, the film star, and that I was after your money!' said John, grinning from ear to ear.

Anyway they gave us a tremendous welcome and I was made to feel very much at home. Sophie was a great big motherly farmer's wife, used to cooking for ten or more every day, and she could chat with me while she did so. John talked farming with Tommy and the boys. Then we had a splendid meal.

We left soon after because of the treacherous roads, and had a contented drive home with many a companionable silence - something not often achieved by me. I felt so easy with this man and hoped our friendship would grow.

Telling Lizzie all about the day and how I felt, I said wistfully 'I wonder what HE was thinking ...'

'He enjoyed every minnit of it,' said she with certainty. 'I could tell by his face. But I'd bet me boots that on the way home he was plannin' what to do with his cattle next day, now he had his trailer back!'

She turned out to be right as usual - but then again, so did I!

Damsel In Distress

Yes, our friendship grew and we got married. It never occurred to us to do anything else, such as co-habiting in the modern fashion. With hindsight, I can appreciate that getting married at our age - I was just into my forties and John was eleven years older - was quite an undertaking, but it didn't seem to worry us at the time.

My first meeting with John was at a local farm auction where he was introduced to me by a mutual friend, Patrick Stokes. I had just bought a pile of old doors for next to nothing. I was examining some useful looking lengths of timber alongside, all of which I planned to use in a shed I was adapting for the cows.

Along came John, and Patrick who said 'You're not planning to buy that, are you Louise?'

I looked surprised, and he took out a pen-knife and dug into one of the pieces and showed me a live "death-watch beetle"! He advised me strongly not to bring this home as it could spread in due course to all my outhouses. I was glad to take their advice on this one but soon became involved again. The auctioneer was selling a very good-looking, well-fitted chicken house at the give-away price of £25 and, although I hadn't planned to buy a chicken house, I couldn't resist raising my hand. To my surprise it was knocked down to me! At first I was delighted, but then was faced with the problem of how to get it home. It was very big - no wonder people weren't bidding for it. But along came Patrick and John again and - yes, you've guessed it - John volunteered to send a tractor and trailer to bring it home for me.

He planned to do this the very next morning, but first there were unforeseen complications. We hadn't realised that the chicken house was wider than the trailer and, indeed, was too wide for the gateway going out of the field. My heart sank. But John was undeterred, took some measurements, and got his tractor man "to-ing and fro-ing" while he watched one tall granite gatepost and I watched the other, and eventually the chicken house squeezed through with an inch to spare on either side! Two inches between success and failure - I took it to be a good omen. Perhaps it wouldn't have made any difference. John loved helping "damsels in distress".

After the next sales day at the Ashford Mart, he invited me to come and see his newly bought Friesian heifers. Patrick came too. He took us into a field down in Cronykeery where we saw a beautiful little Friesian calf coming towards us.

Suddenly, John shouted and ran past the calf towards the mother cow who was following, and turned her away. He kept shouting at us 'Get out, get her out of the field!' Though puzzled we didn't delay and John soon joined us, his face white with fright. After a few moments to catch his breath, he explained that freshly calved cows can be very dangerous, especially if a dog is within sight. She was already charging at me when he managed to block her view and turn her. Patrick and I were so busy admiring the calf that we never saw the danger. I was small and wearing a furry looking brown coat and John thought that she took me for a dog. I was most impressed by his quick thinking and courageous action. John was rising steadily in my estimation.

We began to see a lot of each other, and soon I was consulting him on all farming problems. After the hilarious snowy day at Avoca it wasn't long before we were fixing a day for the wedding - June 1, 1954.

The ceremony was to be held at the Unitarian Church in St. Stephen's Green followed by a reception at Ballinahinch. I wanted the reception to be a simple one at home with just our two families and a few mutual friends, about fifty in all. I wondered whether even this number might be too much to manage on our own, so I asked John would his housekeeper, Mary, like to come and give us a hand. I don't know exactly what message reached her, but when she eventually arrived she was wearing long dangling earrings and high heeled shoes and clearly regarded herself as a guest. But the family plus Lizzie and Bridie rose to the occasion brilliantly. My mother did some lovely flower arrangements and brought out all her best silver, glass and china, with several beautiful, lacey table-cloths to set them off.

I had been afraid that my mother would feel let down by my desertion. After all, she had sold her house in Foxrock when she joined our farming adventure, and built on her own "Granny flat". Here was I, only twenty months later, getting married and departing to live somewhere else! But if she did feel this she never showed it and was as unselfishly supportive as ever.

John Tyner and I pose self-consciously on our wedding day - hold that smile, please! (1954)

They wouldn't let me do anything on the day, which was just as well as I had my own problems to solve. I spent part of the morning walking round and round the yard, hoping that my feet would swell enough to keep my shoes on! I had had to buy them a half size too big to match my outfit, and I was terrified that I might lose them walking up the aisle. In the event I didn't shed my shoes, in fact I'm told that once we were wed John and I flew down the aisle and into the waiting taxi so fast that nobody got a good look at us.

We arrived at Ballinahinch a good half hour earlier than our guests. We put in the time by drinking a bottle of champagne between the three of us - driver included! I was dreading meeting all John's extended family and not knowing which was which, and what to say to them. Now I was able to circulate quite happily asking each one who they were and what was their connection to John, and found it dead easy! Looking at the photographs today it's possible to see the effects of the champagne in each one, and I can truly recommend it! All in all, it was a day to remember.

With a judicious "top-up" we kept all our goodbyes happy, and our departure took place under a cloud of confetti, a lot of which I carried away with me. Apart from an immediate stop to remove a bunch of rattling plough points tied on to the car, all went well and we reached the house in Greystones of our best man, Dr. Tony Mitchell, where we paused to re-organise. I had to apologise to Mrs. Mitchell for all the little piles of confetti we left on the bathroom floor!

Later we boarded the Mail Boat at Dún Laoghaire for the first stage of our honeymoon trip to Portugal. We caught a flight from London to Lisbon. Once there, however, our luck seemed to depart from us entirely. We had planned our trip carefully, as we were afraid that the Algarve in Portugal might be uncomfortably hot in June. If so, we would be able to go to the north of Spain and the cooler regions. It was hot alright, and John, despite warnings, unwisely sat out in the sunshine after a heavy lunch and fell asleep. He had to stay in bed for two days with sunstroke!

When he felt strong enough, we travelled north by train which turned out to be very interesting. John had the satisfaction of seeing for himself that Portuguese farming was backward in comparison with Ireland, and his day was made when he saw a woman pulling the plough with the man just holding the handles! I hastened to point out that he couldn't count on me to do likewise!

Our troubles were not over yet. When we got to the north-west

Escape at last! (1954)

corner of Spain we encountered such cold, unpleasant weather that we didn't have warm enough clothes. We finally decided to change our plans completely and fly to the Costa Brava on the Mediterranean coast, where warmth was guaranteed.

We booked a flight on a small inland airline which would take us right across Spain flying just south of the Pyrenees. There were wonderful mountain views, but the plane was a small, commuter variety which scared me stiff as it made huge bumps and jumps whilst landing at every small town on the way. At last the final hair-raising landing was made, and we and our luggage were permitted to escape. We were transferred to the slowest of slow cross-country buses which stopped at every village collecting farming people and their shopping. We began to wonder what sort of a place we were going to end up in. It did, however, finally deposit us at a very comfortable modern hotel in an attractive little fishing village where we should have been happy. Now it was my turn to take to my bed with a nasty "fluey" cold, and I couldn't enjoy the pleasant heat.

So all things considered we were more than happy to get home and start farming again.

The Stone

Often when I go walking up the fields I pass a large, triangular granite stone lying close to the fence - a beautiful stone shining in the sunlight. I remember very clearly how I met it for the first time.

When I started farming, woman ploughmen - I should say ploughwomen - were scarce. So, for that matter, were women farmers. People wishing to be complimentary, or just making conversation, would tell me 'You must go in for the ploughing championships,' without really thinking it through. This was a keenly contested competition which was held every year, and it included a special competition for women. The winner would be named "Queen of the Plough" for a whole year. So when I married John I already had it in mind.

'Could you teach me how to plough, John, so I can go in for the ploughing contest?'

'Oho! So it's the Queen of the Plough now, is it?' teased John. 'I can do better than that. I'll get Michael D, last year's Wicklow Champion, to come and show you how. It'll be handy as we have quite a bit to do up at Ballinahinch, with the two cornfields.'

He was as good as his word, and one day soon afterwards Michel D arrived in the yard. I watched with interest as he "set" my plough to suit the field we were in, Hollow Field. It was quite a complex procedure as I was to find out for myself, and one I had never realised was necessary. I just thought that one attached the plough and off one went. Now I learned that if the field had been in grass then one turned a shallow sod which rots down and enriches the soil where the seed is sown. If the field was in stubble then a deeper and looser sod was turned to bury the weeds and to present the best tilth for the seed. Hollow Field had been in grass indefinitely, and we expected a heavy crop to result from the beautiful ploughing I would be doing.

'There's really nothing to it,' I thought to myself, as John took Michael D off to celebrate at the local pub. I sailed on full of joy until the fateful moment when I hit the stone!

Gussie the tractor, together with that mad ploughwoman (1955).

To understand what happened one needs to know that most Wicklow farmland is situated on the edge of a great granite plateau. Loose boulders are always apt to surface unexpectedly, as the soil gets eroded by the rain and the boulders are gradually forced up. All one can do is to lift them out by tractor and deposit them in the nearest fence. I had hit one of these enormous stones an almighty whack which resulted in the careful set of my plough being disturbed. I could not manage to get it right again. I had to learn that it requires strong hands and much experience to set even a two furrow plough correctly, and I hadn't the nerve to ask Michel D. to come back again.

Well, Hollow Field did get ploughed eventually, but you could always see the difference after the spot where I had hit the stone. Funnily enough, I never did become "Queen of the Plough"!

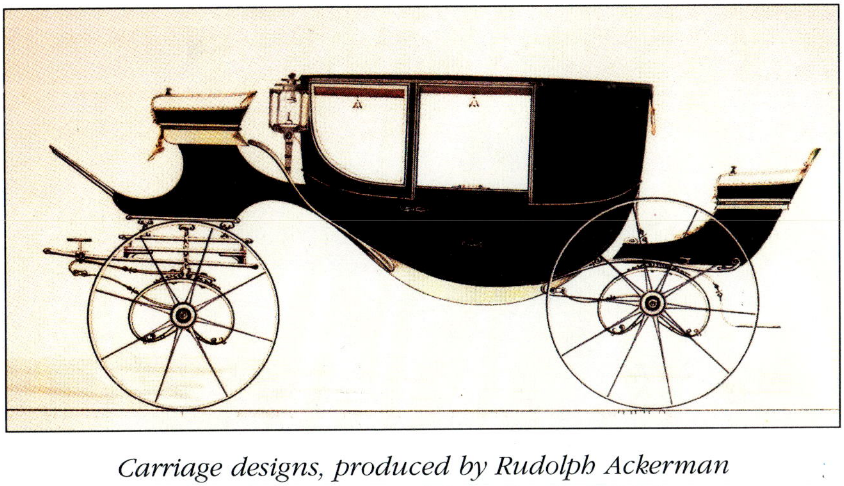

Carriage designs, produced by Rudolph Ackerman for John Hutton and Sons (early 1790s).

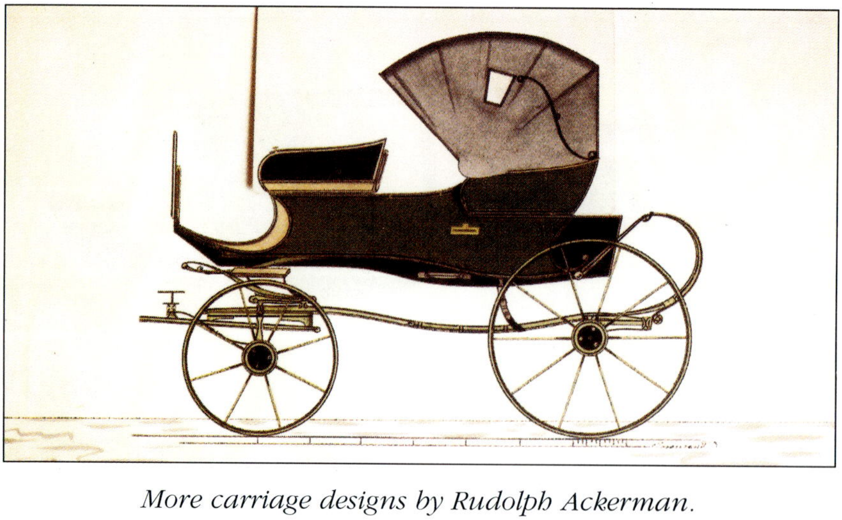

More carriage designs by Rudolph Ackerman.

Henry Hutton,
Lord Mayor of Dublin
in 1803.

Rosa (standing), Priscilla (left) and Annie Hutton,
painted by Frederick Burton (1842).

The Irish State Coach - built by Huttons in 1852 for Queen Victoria.

The Irish State Coach on its way
to the official Opening of Parliament.

Bridie looks after the chickens, Ballinahinch (1962).

Bridie feeds our Kerry calves in the hayshed (1963).

Relaxing in Bumpy Field (1965).

Ness takes a breather, Bumpy Field (1980).

Kevin and Wat (and Ness and Daisy), Hollow Field (1983).

President Hillery, Archbishop Connell and me,
RNLI Lifeboat Launch (1989).

Ballinahinch (1999).

Pip And The Devil's Glen

Pip was a sturdy, rough-coated, salt and pepper cob who belonged to the lady who put farming into my head in the first place. I had ridden him on two or three occasions with her. One day - it must have been in late 1953 - she rang me up.

'How are you for grass down there? I'm asking because I'm very short, and I'd be much obliged if you could take Pip for a while.' She belonged to a "Save the Horses" organisation. 'You could ride him as much as you like.'

I was delighted to agree because I had very few cows as yet, and plenty of grass in hand.

So one fine day Pip arrived by horse-box, and straight away we put him out among the cows. He had a lovely, clean stable with his own supply of hay and an automatic drinker. We could tell he enjoyed it. It was four-star accommodation for him and he settled down well and grew a good heavy coat, so much so that we realised that we would have to "half-clip" him before the spring.

I dug out my old baggy riding breeches and a rather tight riding coat. I liked to take him out on Sunday mornings as I wasn't much of a church goer. Pip knew well when it was Sunday - I'm not sure how - and on that day each week he was much more difficult to catch! Perhaps it was the church bells chiming sweetly across the fields, from Ashford in one direction and from Nun's Cross in the other. Whatever the reason, he certainly did his best to evade me.

I had been told that one certain way to attract a horse, or indeed any animal, is to ignore him completely and to examine something very carefully on the ground. Eventually curiosity will bring him to you. The careful placement of an apple out of which you had taken a bite - thus releasing the lovely scent - on the ground beside you, might result in his head-collar coming within reach of your hand. Thankfully this piece of old motherly advice seemed to work with Pip, although it often took the best part of an hour before I could catch him.

I had had a course of riding lessons at Hume Dudgeon's some time before and knew the essentials, but I had very little experience of riding by myself. Pip knew I was nervous and would act up a bit. He was kind and never did enough to unseat me, but I didn't know when I might expect a sudden jump sideways, or a little unexpected buck. However, we always survived. I could never time my rides to be sure of avoiding the Nun's Cross church goers, many of whom I knew personally, as we made our way past the church on the way to the Devil's Glen. Even if I timed our arrival correctly, we might have to run the gauntlet on the way back. I didn't have a hard hat and was somewhat windblown into the bargain, so we made "a shaggy pair"!

All our difficulties were forgotten when we reached the shelter of the Devil's Glen. This was - and remains - a most beautiful glen through which the little tumbling Vartry river makes its way down from Roundwood Reservoir far above. It plunges over the top of this narrow wooded glen to make a spectacular waterfall. It then rushes noisily on down to the rocky bottom, in a series of little frothy cascades into deep brown pools, dappled by sunshine on the good days. It swirls around mossy rocks, which almost touch the lowest branches of the trees which seem to lean over from the steep sides of the valley. There are many rare trees to be found including the original Irish oaks. With luck, one will catch a sight of a wild Irish deer. I remember especially meeting a beautiful amber-eyed fox face to face - we were both so surprised that we stayed gazing at each other for quite a while before moving. Then there was a flick of his magnificent brush and he was gone!

In season, the banks and hedgerows are richly carpeted with wild flowers such as wood anemones, wild garlic, bluebells, primroses, violets and marvellous mosses and ferns - a truly magical place. To all these ingredients, the reader should add a rather jumpy Pip and his nervous rider! It made a very exciting expedition.

There was one point which we seldom got past. It was just a little drain which crossed the narrow path at right angles. It was no more than a trickle of water about two foot wide, but Pip always stopped and refused to cross it and I couldn't kick hard enough to make him. Occasionally he would make the effort, but mostly we were obliged to turn back and go gently home thinking of Sunday dinner and rewarding oats.

Pip and I soon got used to each other and we enjoyed our outings to the full. Then there came a time when he began to upset the cows, by charging about among them and putting them to flight. I think it was a sort of game to him and just high spirits, but it didn't suit our milking cows. I remember my dismay as I listened to his galloping hoof-beats in Bumpy Field, next door to the house. I didn't have enough grass to give him a field to himself, so I asked John if I could bring him down to Cronykeery and put him in the paddock there for a while. This we did, but the paddock had only one and a half acres in it and Pip had it eaten flat in just one fortnight! My husband was emphatic when he refused to let him mix with any of his cattle - so back to Ballinahinch he had to come.

I realised I'd have to get rid of him. I was planning to sell him to another happy home when his previous owner suddenly rang me up one day to ask me to send him back to her! It was a bit of a shock. By that time I had come to believe he belonged to me, but she had regarded him always as being on loan and she needed him now. I began to see that, although I was sorry to part with him, it would solve all my problems. So very sadly Pip and I had to say "goodbye".

Every time I walk up the Devil's Glen I remember all his little "quirks", especially the spot which he almost always refused to cross.

Garda Monks

It was always difficult to find parking space in Dublin, even before widespread clamping was introduced. But I felt I could usually "get away" with brief halts if I could have a chat with the nearest member of the Garda Siochána.

On one occasion when my husband was busy with the harvest, it must have been in August or September 1965, he asked me to pick up some paint he had ordered from Maguire and Gatchell. This was a shop right in the middle of the city near O'Connell Bridge. I circled the block several times, but could not find a space where I could stop. In the end, I paused near the back door in Pearse Street hoping, that if I was quick enough, I might not be noticed. A vain hope, indeed, because when I got back to the car there was a tall Garda standing over it just getting out his note book. So I rushed up to him, and said 'I hope you are not going to take my number, because I've only been here a couple of minutes while I fetched this paint which was already ordered.'

There was no response, so I went on. 'I tried so hard to find a parking space, but this was the only place I could find to stop.' But he was quite unmoved by any of my protestations.

So finally, in desperation, I said 'And as for you, young man, I think that you should be down the country helping with the harvest, rather than making life difficult for the likes of me in Dublin!'

At which his stern young face broke into a smile, and he stopped writing and replied.

'Oh, if only I could, Ma'am, I'd love to be down there in Wicklow, where I was born. But the fact is that it's the likes of you ladies, Ma'am, who make life so difficult for us up here in Dublin, that prevents me!'

However, I was relieved to see that he was closing his notebook and putting it into his pocket. Then he said 'Gwan 'wid ye, Ma'am, and tell them down in Wicklow that I wasn't too hard on ye, Ma'am!', and he walked away.

'Oh I will, I will!,' I said, and heaved a sigh of relief.

Having got away with it on this occasion, I suppose I gained a sort of false confidence the next time I went to Dublin. However, I hadn't yet met Garda Monks. On this occasion, I was asked to fetch a bag of biscuit meal from Smyth's Market across the river. My husband used to mix it with rat bait to control the rats, which were such a menace during harvest time. I was on my way home, crossing the Liffey by Grattan (or Capel Street) Bridge, when I saw a tall, elderly Garda directing the traffic ahead. I had no sense of impending disaster as I drove quite slowly straight towards him. Unfortunately for me, my right hand indicator was faulty - in those days we only had manually operated indicators which flicked in and out as required. Mine had got stuck pointing out to the right while I drove straight ahead to my doom!

'Oh!' I said, when he stopped me. 'I'm so sorry. I'm afraid it's got stuck.' I tried to free it, half expecting him to give me a hand with it.

But no, he was now prowling slowly around the car taking the number and examining the tax and insurance disks, and then on round the back to see what I was carrying. All this time the traffic was queuing up in all four directions, and he motioned me into the side of the road. There he questioned me as to what was in the bag I was carrying, and whether or not I had a carrier's licence.

'No,' I said, 'I didn't think it was necessary. My husband is a farmer, and I've been carrying the odd sack for him for hundreds of years!'

At this point, he looked so very pleased that I realised my reply hadn't helped! So, when he asked me to produce insurance papers and driving licence I decided that attack was the best defence. I demanded HIS number, to which request he paid no attention at all but just kept on writing in his note-book. Then I got out MY notebook, but he was so tall that I couldn't see his number. So I reached out and up through my window, caught his collar and pulled it down to my level, where I could see it and write it down!

He made no attempt to resist, and finally motioned me on. As I escaped up Parliament Street, I could see him in my mirror still writing away. When I got home to my husband I told him that I was surely going to be summonsed, and we both expected the worst.

Nothing happened for months and I began to wonder had I escaped again. But no such luck. Just a week before Christmas 1965 the summons arrived, and it contained no less than five clauses:

1. Faulty indicator
2. Dangerous driving
3. No carrier's licence
4. No Insurance
5. Assaulting a police officer in the course of his duty.

This last one gave us a bit of a shock. I hadn't expected it, and it alarmed my husband to such an extent that the very next day he took me up to Dublin to see the AA Solicitor, a Mr. Kirwan. He, however, was very comforting, as he said this officer's name was Garda Monks. This particular Garda was well known for the large number of summonses he managed to send in, and for his aggressive attitude, especially towards lady drivers!

'But how did you manage to assault him?' Mr. Kirwan asked.

I explained about the collar pulling. Although he was amused, he said 'I strongly advise you to apologise to Garda Monks.'

'Apologise!?' I said. 'I did apologise at the very beginning, and I'm damned if I'm going to apologise again to that bully!'

'I know how you feel,' said Mr. Kirwan tactfully, 'but if that goes down against you it will be on your driving record for keeps and you never know when it will affect you in the future. It could even affect your husband's good name!' So they both talked me into an apology, much against my will.

In any case, Garda Monks had made a mistake about my supposed lack of insurance. I had shown the relevant papers to him at the time of the incident. I would have to make an appearance in court, but I wasn't to worry as Mr. Kirwan said he would do all the talking.

Once again, there was a long wait, but finally I was summonsed to attend court in Dublin. I became very nervous. I had never been in court before, and I was concerned that I would be asked to make a public apology. If that happened, I wasn't at all certain what I might say if Garda Monks was looking too pleased with himself! So it was with some trepidation that we finally got there, my husband in support.

We sat through several previous cases. Then my case was called. Mr. Kirwan, sitting some distance away up near the judge, went through the various points and finally said that his client, Mrs. Tyner, wished to apologise to Garda Monks. Then Garda Monks, who was sitting on the other side of the court, rose to his feet, said 'Whatever Mr. Kirwan, says IS RIGHT!' and sat down again. And that was that - somewhat of an anti-climax! I was fined five shillings.

We said our "thank yous" to Mr. Kirwan and headed home. There had been no "triumphalism" about Garda Monks when he got up to speak. Perhaps Mr. Kirwan had rubbed in his mistake about my insurance, but I'm very careful what I say to the Gardai now. You'll be pleased to hear that I haven't assaulted one in years!

Aughrim Of The Sorrows

My brother Walter gave me a present of a sheepdog when we started farming. He named him "Mascot" to bring us luck, but somehow he got himself called "Pupser". I don't know why. He wouldn't work for me at all, but attached himself to Bridie whom he perceived, quite rightly, to be doing the actual work. I couldn't persuade him to change his mind. So when I got married and moved down to Cronykeery - my husband's farm - I left him at Ballinahinch with Bridie.

John understood how much I missed Pupser and made good my loss by inviting me to choose a pup from the litter just presented to him by his favourite collie bitch. She had been sired by a very good working dog belonging to the Tyners of Shillelagh. I found it a very difficult choice to make as they were such a lovely lively bunch of pups, all full of fun and "divilment"! However, there was only one bitch among them, which made it easier, as I had determined to make a complete change this time. She was beautiful, with a glossy black coat, pure white shirtfront and a pair of big brown eyes. We called her "Gobbie" after St. Gobnaith, the patron saint of the bees. I think it was because she liked honey.

She was a timid little thing which kept hiding away in a corner. I thought this would be no harm as she might fit in better with the other dogs which were already there. They were all working dogs - spaniels for shooting and Wicklow Collies for the sheep and cattle - all trained by John and devoted to him. He wanted me to have one of my own to keep me company. Gobbie certainly did that, but sadly she was never any good with sheep. She tended to scatter them instead of collecting them. Soon it became apparent that all she wanted was to herd the hens which John kept on free range round the yard. Of course, this wasn't allowed, but she never gave up trying. As she grew bigger and more confident, she would run them to and fro until they dropped from sheer exhaustion and then she would pull their feathers out! It was just fun to her and she didn't mean to kill them, but some of them died, probably from sheer fright!

In the end, John, who loved his birds, said 'If Gobbie kills another hen I'll shoot her in the morning!' I knew he meant it and promised that she wouldn't, and I tried to see that she was kept in her house when I wasn't there. But one day, when I went shopping, she got out and chased and killed another hen. One look at John's face and I knew there would be no reprieve. He promised to take her far away from the house the next morning so that I wouldn't hear the shot.

Daylight came and he was already gone. I buried my tearful face in the pillow but couldn't help listening in spite of myself. I heard nothing. Finally, I heard him come in below and he came up the stairs at once and said 'I found I couldn't do it. She looked up at me so trustingly with her big brown eyes, and she belonged to you!' So she survived and I managed to keep her out of trouble by always taking her with me wherever I went. If John was driving she would curl up at my feet, but this was what finally led her into trouble again when she was quite old.

It was one evening in the autumn of 1968. John was going to fetch some pullets he had seen advertised for sale near Aughrim, about an hour away from us by car. I went along too for the drive. As usual, Gobbie leapt into the car and curled up at my feet. As we drove south the clouds piled up and became blacker and blacker. When we reached Aughrim and pulled up in the village to get petrol, there was a sudden downpour. I was actually in the little shop behind the pumps getting some items for our supper when the heavens opened, and I made a dash for the car with my arms full of groceries. John pulled me and my purchases in out of the rain and we drove off. We found the little farm about ten minutes drive away, and thirty chickens were put into two big crates and then into the back of the car.

As we were about to leave, I asked 'Where's Gobbie?' There was no sign of her and we realised that we must have left her behind at the petrol station. We drove back immediately hoping to find her still there.

There was no sign of Gobbie and nobody had seen her. It was

still pouring with rain. She must have followed me to the shop and when I ran for the car she got left behind. What were we to do? I was beginning to panic. My husband said he must take the chickens home. It wasn't good for them to be left cooped up in the crowded crates. He said that he would come back for me as soon as possible. He gave me his anorak and I set out to search Aughrim on foot for the next hour or so, in the heaviest of heavy rain.

Soon, anorak or not, I was soaked to the skin. I met several barking dogs, some big and menacing, and all sorts and types of people, including some tinkers, but never a sight nor sound of Gobbie. My heart got heavy - heavy as the rain - there was a great bond between us and I was afraid the tinkers had got her. Then John found me, and said 'You're coming home NOW! We can come again tomorrow.' He swept me off home to a hot bath and hot whiskey.

I was so tired that I slept solidly as soon as I got into bed. I awoke the next morning to face searching all the various roads out of Aughrim towards Aughavanna and Tinahely, towards Woodenbridge and Avoca, asking always 'Have you seen a little old collie with a white face - she's very deaf ...?' My niece came with her boys one day to help with the search, and Bridie and Wat from Ballinahinch and my two old friends Mary and Louisa Kent came too, but to no avail. Gobbie had vanished.

Then John got in touch with Clarke Delahunt, the auctioneers, who were holding their usual sale in Aughrim on the coming Monday. That day, they very kindly announced that Mrs. Tyner had lost her old deaf collie to which she was very much attached - and at last we got a result.

There was a big house and farm up above the village owned by a very solitary man. We were told he didn't like people, especially women, or dogs. He did like cats, and he fed a great many in his big old yard. One of his tractor men said he'd seen a dog with this whitish face, sneaking out of the yard in the early morning. So, the next day the search shifted there.

I met the old misogynist and persuaded him to allow us to walk his fields and to search his many outhouses. I thought Gobbie might come again to steal the cats' food. He gave us permission - grudgingly I could see, much against his will - and so we tried to keep out of his sight as we called out 'Gobbie, Gobbie, Gobbie' and blew our whistles non-stop for the next few days.

I was beginning to give up hope. We'd been searching every day for over a week, and I knew she was so timid that she would hide away during the daytime in some hidey-hole. She might get too weak to go looking for food and would never be found. So I decided on one last desperate effort. I asked the man who had seen her last to tell me where that had been exactly. Then I went home and got my own very old brown coat, and a large bowl of milk to which John added a beautiful juicy bone. I went back down in the evening and put them at the identified spot and asked your man to look there in the early morning. I promised that if this failed we wouldn't be troubling them again. Then I went home with a heavy heart thinking I wouldn't be seeing Gobbie again. But they rang me up quite early in the morning to tell me that Gobbie had been found fast asleep on my coat!

It didn't take me long to get back down there to collect her. Our host had shut her into a room and warned me to keep the door shut 'as she might run away again ...' Of course, this was quite unnecessary whilst I was there. Gobbie had lost half her weight during the week's semi-starvation, and I could lift her easily all a-tremble in my arms as I put her into the car. I said all my "thank-yous" and could see the relief in my host's face when we took off joyfully for home. We got a great welcome from all who had helped us during that hardship of a week.

There was a bit of dirty old twine still tied round Gobbie's neck, and a trailing bit which she had obviously chewed through to make her escape. Someone had tied her up for a time, perhaps waiting for a reward to be offered. 'Much more likely to have been yer man,' said John, 'if he caught her disturbing his cats'. However, I was so grateful to him for allowing us to find her that I wrote him a beautiful letter full of thanks and appreciation. Naturally enough, I never got an answer!

Meanwhile, Gobbie put on weight again and lived another two years before dying peacefully in her own bed.

On My Eighty-Fourth Birthday In November

I leant against a sunny wall
And a butterfly lit on my toe.
I didn't dare move a muscle then
Lest it would flutter and go.

'Why did you wait for this special day?
Did you know I was eighty-four?'
The beech leaves are falling on my head
And the summer flowers are no more.

'Why are your brilliant wings so large
For your slender body to lift?'
For scientists probing the "Chaos Theory"
Butterfly shape is a gift.

For with seemingly random ripples and breezes
Nothing's now left to chance.
If my butterfly flutters its wings right here
It could cause a storm in France!

When I'm one hundred and eighty-four
I hope I can lean on that wall
And the butterfly comes as it did before
And the beech leaves continue to fall.

John and one of his Prize Bullocks, Ashford Mart (late 1950s). John attended the cattle sales every Monday, and was a member of the Livestock Committee for years.

Ness And The Hunt

The hunt was going to cross my husband's farm at Cronykeery and I was keen to get some photographs. This was our local "drag hunt" which meant there would be no chasing or killing of animals.

John was busy on the potato harvester when I called up to him. 'Is it all right to go up the Hill with Ness to take some snapshots?'

'Yes,' he replied, 'If you want to. But take care to keep clear of them. We don't want any further trouble. I've already moved the cattle.'

The last time the hunt came across our fields they had suddenly changed course and tangled with the cattle. Perhaps the hounds had picked up the scent of a real fox. In any case, the cattle panicked and scattered in all directions, which wasn't good for them nor for the hedges they charged through! This time they had been put into the safety of the cattle-yard with some hay to keep them happy.

"The Hill" rose sharply behind the house to a height of some 200 to 300 feet. I was in the habit of climbing it most days, partly for my figure but mostly for the magnificent view it afforded from the top. One could see to the sea and Wales in one direction, and to the Wicklow Mountains in the other. From the stream at the bottom I could climb it in about twenty minutes at my pace, which suited that of Ness, a young sheep-dog, who was also putting on weight and who usually came with me. She hadn't been out of her house for a few days because she was "in season". She had gone a bit lame in her hind-quarters and I knew that we both needed the exercise.

I planned to be up on top of the Hill well in advance of the hunt proper, but in time to watch for the man carrying "the drag". He rode ahead laying the scent for the hounds to follow some ten or twenty minutes later. In this way, I would know exactly where they would pass and could position myself to the best advantage, at a safe distance.

All went according to plan - at first. I was sitting tucked in beneath a handy gorse bush, with Ness stretched out beside me in the warm sunshine. We could both smell the heady scent of the gorse flowers and enjoy the wide view of the countryside spread out below. The hunt was already in sight like a scarlet thread as they trotted up our lane, and then broke into a gallop as they followed the hounds across the open fields. I had my camera up and focussed on one of the small green fields below us, and in a excited rush they were there. The hounds broke through and seemed to pause and circle as they picked up the scent again. I waited until the huntsmen joined them, and was just about to press the shutter when - suddenly - a dark shape streaked across the lens. It was Ness rushing full tilt down the Hill to join the hounds!

Ness considers whether to live up to her responsibilities, or join her new play mates (1972). You can just about make out the hunt approaching in the middle distance.

She was quite deaf to my frantic efforts to call her back. I had clean forgotten that she was still "in season". I ran down after her as fast as I could but she was already in the midst of the clamorous hounds. There was a very irate huntsman circling them on a very large horse, cracking his long whip as he tried to regain control of his pack. He focussed his attention on me and loudly instructed me to take my so-and-so bitch away. All this time more and more riders arrived and joined the *melée*, anxious to see what the hounds had caught!

Meanwhile, Ness was enjoying herself quite unashamedly as the centre of so much "doggy" attention. She avoided easily all my attempts to catch her. I felt about ten inches tall with all these people looking down at me from their huge horses. I had been told to keep clear of the hunt and here was I right in the middle of it and most unpopular! I could imagine what John was going to say.

Finally, I managed to get the lead onto Ness that should have been there from the start. She wouldn't budge, however much I tugged, but gradually the hounds were brought under control and they moved away. The riders followed, some of them obviously disapproving, but more of them amused at my predicament.

I went dejectedly to find John and to own up to my latest misfortune.

Suddenly he started to laugh. 'Will you look at Ness now?' and I saw her fairly gambolling around him, quite rejuvenated, and with not a suspicion of a limp.

'Wonderful what a little bit of sex can do for you, isn't it?' said he - and suddenly I was laughing too.

When I Reached Eighty-Five

I sat upon a cloudlet in my old blue dressing-gown
The sunshine poured around me from the blue, blue sky
The phone brought loving talk from faraway Hong Kong
Peter said 'You've made it, keep it up 'til I get there.'
Margaret brought a present - she said it wasn't good
    enough
I loved her rosy red wind-chime of tiny bells and pearls
It's hung where every breeze will make it sweetly play.
My dog and I then floated round the beauty of the fields
The postman brought me comfort - I hadn't lost old friends
The English phone brought Clare reminiscing of old times
When Reg, her husband, shared with me the very same
    birthday
And she had double trouble from two Scorpios at once!

Today I had no trouble having fixed my tea at Hunter's
Where new groups met with older friends
Together giving pleasure with cards and wish-me-wells.
Then they hushed to drink my health
As Cherry's singing candle added magic to her cake.
It sang the "Happy Birthday" song as plain as plain could be
Then Albert made a speech about the Irish coach and me
How it was renovated the same year I was born.
I won't forget my 85th - it made me feel reborn!

Five Acres

John and I were down in one of his fields in Cronykeery, making a list of how much seed wheat we would need to sow it. Funnily enough, the field was called "Five Acres", not to be confused with the "Four Acres" we had in Ballinahinch. It was a flat, richly fertile little field surrounded by larger fields and the nearby bog.

'Ten acres,' said John, and, seeing my puzzled face, he continued.

'It's a misleading title because it's five IRISH acres which is the equal of eight STATUTE acres, and more in this case. I have to remember the two acres I added in when I started draining "the Bog". That year I only ordered enough seed to do the eight acres and had to leave the two in grass!'

'So "Five Acres" is really ten acres!' went on John. 'It all started when Toddy Sullivan got mixed up following the visit of the Department's drainage expert who came and pegged it out for us. The ground is so flat, ye see, that there's very little fall. Toddy was to dig the drains from one peg down to another and so on - but either one peg got lost or he didn't see it and he linked them up wrong all the way. Like you would do up your cardigan askew with a button to spare at the bottom. So Toddy put in the right number of drainpipes all right but there was no fall on them, so they didn't drain - naturally ...'

'That's as clear as mud!' I said.

'Precisely,' said John. 'We had to take them all up again!'

On Sundays, John and I loved to walk through the fields at Cronykeery as he planned the next week's work. During the winter it would be the next set of drains to be dug. Toddy Sullivan was long gone when I arrived on the scene, but by that time John had acquired Tom White - a truly wonderful digger of drains.

I have a clear picture in my mind of Tom as he stood knee-deep in his 12" wide drain digging away like a cheery old mole, never seeming to tire. Once I asked John 'Why don't you get a digger for the tractor?'

'As long as I have a human digger of the calibre of Tom I don't need a mechanical one,' he replied.

Of course, Tom was very special. When he took on a job, he liked to get it finished, no matter what the hour. As a result he wasn't very popular with the other men who worked by the clock. They went home at six o'clock regardless, or earlier when the light went and it got dark. Tom would try to finish the job and worked on as long as he could.

When John died in 1973, Tom transferred his loyalty to me. He did anything that I wanted doing, be it at Cronykeery or at Ballinahinch. One day, I found Tom working away in the yard at Cronykeery. There were tears streaming down his face.

'What's wrong, Tom?' I asked. 'Are you missing him as I do?'

'Oh Ma'am, I do,' he replied. 'I keep thinking I'll see him come round the corner any minute!'

I didn't have to tell him that I felt the same. We never mentioned it again, but we knew that John was often with us.

Tom used to travel to and fro by bicycle, and I noticed that he tended to be late getting to Ballinahinch. I offered to pick him up by car instead. One day, when I arrived at his home a bit earlier than usual, I found Tom returning from Wicklow on his bike. I asked him why he was going there so early.

'Well, Ma'am,' he said, 'Sally Nuzum has lost her husband, and she needs to keep her garden goin'. I go there first thing every day.'

Sally used to be a Clements living near me at Ashford, and Tom had done all his early work with the Clements. Now that Sally needed help, Tom would get up two or three hours earlier and would work in her garden before coming on to mine. This was typical of Tom's determination to help others - it should be noted that he was in his late sixties at the time.

I paid Tom what I thought was fair. He would never tell me how much that should be. He just said 'Ah! Don't worry, Ma'am, I don't mind. Just give me what ye think!' This was irritating sometimes, as I didn't know what I should give him now that I was fetching him to and fro, but very typical of his good nature.

Oh yes, he was very special, was Tom.

Anyway, in "Five Acres" the whole bog was drained and in lovely grass just two or three short years later. John also took a great deal of trouble planting a hedge round the whole field, incorporating some well-established trees. It made a sort of green oasis amidst the more ordinary big fields around. So, almost thirty years later, when his grandson, Angus, was about to get married, what was more natural than that he and Kim should choose this oasis in which to erect their new house?

'You'll never get it up in time for the wedding,' I ventured and was shot down.

'It'll be up next Tuesday,' said Angus. 'The foundation was ready a week ago with built in heating and Kim has the garden planted already!'

And they invited me to come on Tuesday to see for myself.

It came by lorry at 7 a.m. and was up and keeping out the rain by the evening. Can you imagine it? A whole three-bedroom house, packed on one lorry, all the way from Norway via Galway in the West, with five men who knew how to put it together.

A new interpretation of "mobile home"? (1998)

Of course, the concrete foundation had been laid some time previously and was all measured and ready to receive this house to exact dimensions. The walls, complete with triple-glazed windows, were standing securely in place by 9.30 a.m. and the roof was beginning to go on. We watched fascinated from the plastic tunnel which had been so thoughtfully erected in the garden.

About six hours later, and the house starts to take shape (1998).

This young couple are vegetarians and once the house was planned they lost no time in making the garden, and planting the vegetables and fruit trees that they would need. Early tomatoes were already growing well in the tunnel together with beans, cabbage, broccoli - you name it, they had it. There were also flowers in full bloom which were not only pretty, but which were really designed to attract beneficial insects into the protective tunnel. The paths were lined with stones, this time designed to store the heat of the sun and radiate it again after dark thus defeating the frost! Perhaps a little bit optimistic this, but we were all very impressed by their knowledgeable industry. We were even more impressed when we discovered the orchard behind the tunnel which was already planted with thriving young fruit trees - apples, pears, plums and others. We could imagine how beautiful they would all look in a few years time.

The ironic thing was that Angus planned to construct a lake just across from the house. This lake was situated right in that corner of the field which I have referred to previously as "the Bog". All that hard work over many years to drain the wet land would be reversed. The 1960s doctrine which dictated that every inch of land should be utilised had given way to a softer, more eco-friendly way of farming. The lake would provide a resting place for the many birds which passed that way on their long migratory journeys. The stream would deliver many small fish, such as sticklebacks and common eels, and the watery habitat would support many small insects and, subsequently, many more small birds. Angus and Kim are both keen bird-watchers and this wildlife sanctuary would provide them with many hours of enjoyable pastime.

Various members of both families - Hopkins and Tyners - had turned up to see the speedy progress. We were all given mugs of very welcome hot tea in the tunnel, while we heard what remained to be done after the five men team had finished erecting inner walls and the exciting moment when they handed over the key! A ditch would have to be dug beside the long avenue winding up from the road and into this would go all the pipes bringing water, electricity and telephone - and perhaps drains? Inside the house all these things had to be connected and plugged in, and then all the *décor* and furnishings had to be planned and completed.

Much time and effort still remained to be lavished on this attractive home, but nothing, to my mind, could take away from the initial miracle - when a house was built in a day!

Magpies

I like to count Magpies, those elegant birds:
They can tell me what I want to know.
But it's swallows that swoop as they feed on the wing,
At a speed that makes all else seem slow.
For I'm out in the midst of a field of green corn,
So level it seems solid on top
Till a breeze comes and ripples it like a green lake.
How many fresh loaves in this crop?
The young "shooting" ears of the wheat
Show great promise, given the weather.
It can't be too dry, or too cold and wet -
It's nature and farmer together.

The sunshine's so warm that I've "cast my clout"
Now the Maytree's laden with bloom.
There's a buzzing of bees as the lilac and gorse
Mingle their rich perfume.
Above are the tender new leaves of the trees
Held back by the bitter cold spring.
At foot shining buttercups - speedwell's blue eye
Single magpies a warning bring.

Standing here I feel centred in plenty
Good husbandry seen at it's best.
One magpie's for sorrow, but two are for joy
Surely one will be minding the nest!
So though fear lurks beneath perfect moments
Put it out in full view on the shelf
With other dark thoughts, and enjoy in their place
Inward Grace that lights up the Self.

Ness When She Got Lost

Ness had another adventure in her old age - this time at Ballinahinch. She outlived my husband, John, by several years. She was the last sheep dog he ever had and so was doubly dear to me. She was very good at her job, if a bit slow.

I remember watching when she was sent to collect the sheep at the top of "the Hill" at Cronykeery. We would lose sight of her completely as she circled wide around the edge of the two fields on the way up, taking far too long - unnecessarily long in my husband's view - but he could never get her to go more directly. She always got them in the end if one had the patience to wait. John would walk up the Hill in the meanwhile, and eventually would find the sheep collecting and moving gently downhill towards him as if by magic, with no sign of the dog behind. She would bring them right up to John, and hold them there while he counted or examined them. Then, with her help, he would be able to split them into two flocks, or pick out a lame or sick sheep and bring it with a few companions down to the yard for attention. She would even work for me on occasion and was the only one of his dogs who would. He always trained his dogs in his own special intuitive way - there was no special system of commands - only some penetrating whistles when she was at a distance, plus arm movements to show right or left.

When John died, Ness lived on with me at Ballinahinch. I was happy to have her. She had such a lovely temperament. But as she got older, she got even slower and very deaf. The only way to stop her, if she had a mind to go the wrong way, was to head her off by touch, or to keep her on a lead.

One day, two of my oldest friends, Mary and Louisa Kent, came to tea. Soon after they arrived, I took them and the dogs for a walk up the fields which they loved doing. But then it began to look like rain so we turned for home. It was at that moment that the cattle found us and began to follow behind us. They were only young playful heifers and meant no harm, but they can give one a powerful "dunk" by mistake and I kept on shooing them away until I got Mary and Louisa safely behind a gate.

It was only then that Mary said 'Where's Ness?' and I realised that she wasn't with us. I went back to look for her while my guests went in to put the kettle on. But I couldn't find her.

Nor could we find her later on after tea, when we searched all the hedges where she could be sheltering. I reckoned she must have gone through the nearby hedge and into the corn in Chance Field. True enough, we found a small gap and a pathway leading into the corn which was now tall enough to hide her completely. In addition to this, Louisa said she had heard a dog whining down at the corner of the wheat, but that was near a neighbour's fence and she couldn't tell if it was Ness. By this time the rain was pouring down in torrents, and I insisted on taking Mary and Louisa home to change their wet clothes.

Supper time came and there was still no sign of Ness. I knew she was too old to leave out all night soaked to the skin as she must be. Up to this time, we had only searched the little paths already made by her in the cornfield. I suddenly came to the decision that I would quarter the field systematically, even if I knocked down more wheat. It was still pouring with rain and I was also soaked to the skin, but fortunately it wasn't long before I came upon what looked like a sodden hearth-rug, with two big brown eyes looking trustfully up at me. She was so weak she couldn't stand, but I managed to pick her up, heavy as she was. I couldn't get my voice to work for a while with the lump in my throat, but soon was able to shout 'I've got her, I've got her!' to the other searchers. I staggered out, as my tears mixed with the rain running down my face. Then help came and we got her in and dried in the warm kitchen.

After a warm feed Ness began to recover, but, in a real sense, I never did. I knew then that, given similar circumstances, I would always sacrifice the harvest rather than the welfare of my beloved animals!

Christ Church Cathedral

"Within this hallowed space you may forget the ceaseless activity of daily life and be still"

So reads the Christ Church programme for Choral Evensong and the Installation of Canons which I attended last Sunday. Our own Church of Ireland minister was to be made a canon, and we arrived early to get good seats. We went up near the reredos screening the choir, where they were still busy practising the anthem for the service to come. The great organ was going "full belt" and the strong choir was holding its own.

I was immediately "grabbed" by this powerful music. It was a modern piece by Edward Bairstow, full of discords but also rich in lovely sounds which I found very moving. It certainly suggested the turmoil of daily life. The cathedral had got this new organ only a few months beforehand. It had wonderful deep-down notes which satisfied the soul and which helped to fill this ancient building to the brim. I was surprised to see that there were no boys in the choir, only girls - whose voices could soar with ease to the heights - and, of course, men choristers. I was enthralled and didn't want them to stop, which they had to when it was time for them to form the procession.

The procession consisted of the choristers, followed by the canons-to-be supported by the Archbishop of Dublin. It started off down one of the side-aisles, and then progressed up the centre aisle to the point where the many-arched reredos, with its Golden Door, stopped it from entering the choir area. Here the three canons-to-be were left on our side of the Golden Door, while the choristers took their seats and the Archbishop reached the high altar. Each canon-to-be was then required, one by one, to remake his vows to the church and to sign a declaration to that effect. Only then was he taken gently by the hand, through the Golden Door and up to the high altar where he was welcomed by the Archbishop. Finally, he was shown to his own chair. The canons' chairs are located on either side of the choir, behind the choir stalls. Each canon is allocated his own chair which henceforth can not be used by anybody else.

Meanwhile we had time to relax and lean back, in order to look upwards at the slender pillars supporting the arched roof away up above us. How,' I wondered, 'did the medieval builders build these huge over-tall cathedrals? They had no tractors or machinery to help them. Why did they do it at all? Was it just to get nearer to heaven, or was it in the hope of attracting God into His House and away from His draughty old holy mountains!?'

It was quite a long service. So much so that afterwards I needed to descend into the crypt in search of a toilet. I was further impressed by the evident age of this remarkable building. There has been worship here since the 11th century but the present church was mostly re-erected in the 14th and 15th centuries. The crypt was quite dry, and warm, and apart from a few tombs there was nothing but the ancient pillars supporting the huge edifice above, each of which had a few loose rocks piled round its base.

I had been given tea and buns down here on previous occasions, one of which I remember especially. A few years earlier they had had a Flower Festival and the whole cathedral was decorated most beautifully. The flowers didn't hide anything, rather they accentuated the architecture. They used tiny posies of small wild flowers, such as primroses or daisies, to enrich the mouldings and architraves, but I noticed that no-one had risked offending the fairies by bringing in the mayflowers. I supposed that in God's own house it probably would have been safe enough!

More sophisticated flowers were used to create beautiful arrangements, each of which represented a region served by Christ Church. On that occasion, the pews had been removed from the central aisle to allow a vast mosaic of seeds and grains and flower petals to carpet the stone floor. People came from far and wide to see it all, and gladly replenished cathedral funds which were badly needed for further repairs.

It was while I was turning my handbag upside down on one of the tombs in order to find the requisite 10p for the toilet door that I suddenly had a terrible thought. What would it have been like if I had been down here on Christmas Eve when the ESB turned off the electricity during the storm? Would I ever have been able to find my way back to the world above? Difficult enough with the lights ON, I thought.

I promised myself that next time I would bring a torch!

"Four and twenty blackbirds, baked in a pie ...",
Wicklow Garden Fête (1990).

Wasps' Nest

I was stung on the lip by a wasp and was feeling very sorry for myself. One side of my face swelled up like half a football. Thank goodness it wasn't inside my mouth or I might not be writing this!

We had been clearing the shrubbery of unwanted weeds - Robin-Run-in-the-Hedge and a huge invasion of Convolvulus - when I came upon the wasps' nest. It was just a small hole in the ground which you wouldn't notice if the angry wasps hadn't started circling round my head. Suddenly, one *kamikaze* wasp stung my hand through my gardening glove! While I tried to deal with him another got through to my face. I retreated hastily with still other wasps circling, and got rid of them by shedding my anorak as I fled into the house and slammed the door!

The hum of angry wasps is frightening in the extreme, especially to my dog who dreads them. When we found a second nest in a different part of the shrubbery, I knew that I had to get rid of them. I took the advice of the man who sold me the powder that I would be puffing into the nests. He said I should wait until the evening when all the travellers would have returned home. So I went to look at them about 6 p.m. I approached very gingerly but found them still working hard. I was able to get quite close, as this time I wasn't molesting them and they took no notice of me. I could hear one "zing" past my ear every three or four seconds, then circle the hole once or twice before descending into it on the wing with the greatest accuracy, like a little helicopter. Then another would emerge immediately and "zing" past my other ear on the outward journey, with such perfect timing that they never interfered with each other. They worked with all the precision of an aircraft carrier, with only this comparatively small landing area. I was enthralled by their non-stop performance.

Did they never tire? They must have been at it since dawn. Who or what organises them? Like the bees they respond to chemical signals - but who sends these out? Who sent out the "soldiers" - or the pilots? - to attack me? Suddenly I felt very small and found that I didn't want to destroy this perfect organisation. I went back inside to my tea, very uncertain of my intentions.

Then my dog looked at me with her beautiful, knowing brown eyes which said 'What about me when one of those striped monsters gets into my coat?' I realised the shrubbery just wasn't our own while they were there. So about 8 p.m. when it was dusk, I crept out, found the two holes by torch light and puffed the lethal powder in. I fully expected them to erupt in protest and to attack me, but there was no resistance. I felt like a murderer.

In the morning there was no life and the holes rapidly filled up with fallen leaves.

Scotland The Brave (Post Script)

The telephone brought me another joyful link with my past - the third within the year. This time it was a deep resonant male voice.

'Is that you, Louise? This is Douglas Campbell.' I was dumbfounded, hardly believing my ears.

'No!' I exclaimed.

'Yes, really,' he said, and now I could detect the Scottish "burr" in his voice. 'How are you? I'm here in Ireland. Can I come and see you?'

Then some pips went. 'Sorry, I have to put some money in.' While he fed the phone I got my breath back.

It was such a long time since we had last seen each other. When we had time to count we reckoned it was more than fifty years since we were both in the Citizens' Theatre in Glasgow. It was in 1945 soon after the end of the war. Strangely enough, it wasn't long since I had written up all I could remember about those times, and here was Dougie in person to confirm all I had recorded, and hopefully some more. What a thrill!

I rushed off to find out what I had said about him, and found to my relief that I had been very complimentary. I had been talking about the company's juvenile leads, and that Douglas Campbell was my ideal of a young Scot who should always wear a kilt even if he happened to be living in Sassanach London!

I read it out to him and his wife and the mutual friends who had brought them. I'm afraid it was my terrible lapse when I failed to attend a *matinée*, described previously, that he remembered most clearly about me. However, when I reminded him of the "Razor Gangs" who used to operate in the Gorbals, and also our lovely Sunday excursions to nearby Loch Lomond when he acted as guide, lots of other memories came back to him and we began to recognise each other.

Physically we had both changed with the years. He had developed into a big, heavy man with pure white hair, and I am mostly grey and stooped. We wouldn't have recognised each other in the street, but being of the theatre we both remembered the parts the other had played and the various plays we were in.

The following day, they brought me beautiful flowers and took me to lunch at Hunter's Hotel. They built up my self-esteem to such a point that it took days for my feet to touch the ground again! One tends to take the telephone for granted these days, but now every time I pick it up I wonder which exciting person from my past will I be talking to next!

Mary And Louisa And The RNLI

Mary and Louisa Kent became my very good friends, more or less at the time I married John. When we returned home from our honeymoon, he said that I must meet the Kents immediately. I gathered that they were very special people. John and I were church-goers at the time which made it easy. Not that we were full-blown believers in the Christian story, but we both loved singing in the church choir.

Mary and Louisa's house was quite near the Protestant church in Wicklow, and we were all invited to call in for a cup of tea after the Sunday service. New members were discovered by Louisa who had a gift for bringing us all together. While Louisa socialised, Mary would make the tea and butter the scones. They gave everybody a warm welcome, whether on Sunday or on any other day.

'Ah, there you are, honey!' Mary would say. 'Come right in and tell us all the news.'

It was just the sort of welcome I needed, being so desperately shy. Soon I was calling in every time I went to Wicklow, and if I didn't turn up they wanted to know why.

Mary and Louisa both loved babies. They were happy to baby-sit for anyone who had one, be they Protestant, Catholic or any other belief. There was always at least one of them at home, with perhaps a baby or two keeping warm in the tiny kitchen situated in the back of their house. Louisa might be beating up eggs to make a sponge cake to bring to someone who was ill, whilst Mary would be preparing their own meal.

Soon they had me involved in various church events, including the Garden Fête. Knowing that I had been in the theatre, they were dying for me to supply new and original ideas, and they were even prepared to take on all the extra work entailed in carrying them out. One of the most successful was when we introduced dancing around the maypole, which was followed by an Irish version the next year. This was nearly thirty years before *Riverdance* created so much interest. They loved Wicklow's stoney beach, and taught me how to recognise the semi-precious stones with which it abounds. We spent many happy hours there, even enjoying swimming in the rather cold sea.

Louisa and Mary on The Murrough, Wicklow (1974).

Christmas was a busy time for all of us, but especially so for Mary and Louisa who had such a long list of friends with whom to stay in touch. I tried to time my visits so that I could give them a lift, either down to the shops or back. They lived at the top of the hill beside the church and didn't have a car. Often Mary would walk down and back up twice or three times in one day. She said that it didn't bother her, but I remember clearly her last Christmas with us.

I discovered her searching Hopkins' bargain basement for the sort of presents she and Louisa could afford. I told her that I would drive her and her purchases back home as soon as she had finished. Suddenly, she put her head on my shoulder for a moment, and said, 'I could do with that - I am so tired.' It was the following summer that she fell ill and died. I miss her so much.

Mary had been President of the Ladies Guild of the RNLI for many years. When she died, Louisa didn't want to take it on and she nominated me for the job. That's how I acquired this very special photograph of myself with the Archbishop of Dublin (now Cardinal), the Right Reverend Desmond Connell, and the President of Ireland, Dr. Patrick Hillery. It's an unusual photograph because I am doing the talking and they are doing the listening for a change!

It was Saturday afternoon, September 30, 1989. About half-an-hour later I would be sharing a trip out to sea, with the President, in Wicklow's new lifeboat! Yes, it was the naming ceremony, and as the Ladies' President it was my job to welcome all the VIPs. These included Mr. and Mrs. Vernon from the RNLI head office in Poole, Dorset. Mr. Vernon would be doing the actual naming.

A new lifeboat is usually given the name of it's donor. In this instance it was *The Annie Blaker*. She was a wealthy landowner who had bequeathed a significant amount of money to the Institution. We were told that it was the latest model which could automatically right itself if it capsized, no matter how stormy the sea. Very comforting for the crew, all of whom were volunteers, except for their engineer.

It's amazing to realise that it is now more than 175 years since the RNLI was started. In 1824, a pamphlet entitled "An Appeal To The British Nation" was published by a certain Sir William Hillery. In it he proposed a national lifeboat service which would be paid for by voluntary contributions and manned by voluntary crews. Hillery had witnessed many ships being wrecked at sea, close to but so far away from the help watching on the shore, and it is said that he had rescued many of the survivors himself. Subsequently, he established one of the first lifeboat stations on the Isle of Man, and won several awards from the Institution for his gallantry. The title Royal National Lifeboat Institution was adopted in 1854.

It is sobering to think about how many times the lifeboats have gone out in dreadful weather, and how many lives have been saved. At the time of writing, the number stood at more than 250,000, which included all the launches from all the lifeboat stations in the British Isles and Ireland. This is almost unbelievable given that it had been achieved using only voluntary contributions.

I remember so well a particularly dark and stormy night when the Wicklow Choir, to which I belonged, was rehearsing up at the Dominican convent. A message came through that the lifeboat was going out. Quite a number of our men singers rose up and disappeared out into the night. Our prayers went with them - I

The Annie Blaker *gets officially launched from the east pier, Wicklow (1989).*

thought that they were so brave. It had been bad enough to get to the choir practice on such a night without having to venture out onto the stormy sea!

Thankfully, on the day of the naming ceremony the weather was wonderful. This was just as well, as we had about 500 invited guests from all the Irish lifeboat stations and some from England as well. They all had to be seated on the pier beside the lifeboat house, together with the several church choirs taking part in the service which was a part of the programme.

After all the speeches and other formalities we were taken aboard the lifeboat, which was then launched. I had managed to hide my large hat beside the steerage, and I put on the scarf that I had brought. I held on tightly as we hit the water. I happened to look up at the man doing the steering and recognised the President. He looked down and smiled at me.

'Is it yourself?' I asked.

'Yes, it's myself.'

'Oh,' I said, 'I didn't know you could sail a boat!'

'Neither did I,' he replied. 'It's the first time I've ever done so! Isn't it lovely!'

And indeed it was. We were outside the harbour by this time, and Archbishop Connell had also been offered a chance to steer. He had turned it down to start with, as he said he didn't know how. But when the skipper was taking over before returning to the harbour, he changed his mind.

He said 'If he can do it' - (i.e.the President) - 'So can I!'

The result was that we carried on a bit further out to sea before heading for home.

There we crossed over to the far side of the harbour, where my Ladies Guild members had laid on tea under cover for everyone. I had done my bit by bringing in a large plate of sandwiches in the morning. But now, in the afternoon, I was not allowed to lift a finger. They treated me as another VIP and so I had a wonderful ending to a wonderful day which I'll never forget.

Snowdrop

Rich chocolate-brown of soil fresh ploughed
    Against the blue-black hill,
Beside is glowing green of grass
    Still growing. Strong colours fill
The eye - strong to cope with death,
    With seeming death -
As I tread the rustling leaves
    Blown from rattling skeleton trees,
The ground grows hard each shortening day.
Birds fluff-out or they may freeze
    As does my frosted breath,
Will the sun come back this way?
    Age-old question - leap of faith -
Faith of those who built Newgrange -
    They could plan the very day.
Perhaps they knew that secretly
    New buds had formed that hidden lay,
And if further proof were needed
    Early snowdrops had succeeded,
Pushing up through frozen ground.
    This beauty of design sublime
Is messenger of truth profound -
    Life's indestructable but must change -
Comforting to such as I
Living now on "borrowed time".

Our Daily Bread

"Give us our daily bread ..."

I wonder how often we stop to think how that comes about. First, the seed has to be saved from the year before. Farmers usually buy in new seed as it should be more productive in our soil, and more resistant to disease. However, we have to be sure our suppliers are well-known to be reliable, as otherwise we might be importing new weeds or new diseases. We also have to ensure that the crop from which the seed is taken is well grown, and all of one kind.

Meanwhile, the field has to be ploughed as soon as possible after the previous harvest. It could be in stubble which is the easiest. However, turning the sods of a field which has been in grass for several years is best of all, as long as they are ploughed at the end of the previous season. This gives them time to be broken down by the frost over the winter before being harrowed. Harrowing is coarse to start with, becoming finer each time until a beautiful level tilth is achieved, and then the seed drill goes into action.

I remember my feeling of disbelief that all this seed sown so neatly would actually come up, especially after the heavy ridged three-piece roller flattened it all down tight. I was fascinated when, in two or three days time, my husband would uncover a small part of a drill with his finger to show me the seed already sprouting little green shoots. Soon they were all above ground in neat rows all over the field. I watched them increase and grow and tiller out until there was no space between the stalks.

Now, you might think there was nothing left to do before the harvest but you would be wrong. Wheat has to be watched and sprayed several times - sometimes for weeds, sometimes to control growth so that the straw can become stronger and less likely to lodge, and sometimes for disease especially if the weather persists in being drizzly wet.

Eventually, the colour of the crop will change and each head will start to bend over in preparation for shedding the ripened seed. At this stage, the weather has to be kind to allow the corn to dry, after which it has to be cut. The whole crop can be lost if the rain goes on too long or the wind blows too hard.

Once, I remember, we grew a crop of wheat in High Field at Ballinahinch, where a strong wind was at its worst. I was afraid that the combine wouldn't get it cut before all the grain was shed upon the ground. I was so anxious that I kept running around the edge of the corn, after the combine, in order to see how much of it was already on the ground - though what good that would have done I can't imagine! To my amazement, although the wind did its worst, it held off and the combine gathered it all in with practically no loss.

On another occasion, it was so wet that my wheat at Ballinahinch began to sprout on the stalk. At that time, we still had to put the grain into big sacks tied with string which was knotted by hand. Afterwards, they could be left standing in the field for some time without risk. They were so heavy when full that it needed two men to lift them onto the trailer so that they could be sent into the corn merchant. To my horror and disbelief, on this occasion my trailer load came back to me that same evening. It had never been unloaded as it was deemed to be too far sprouted to be accepted. I had nowhere to put it under cover and anyway the other men had gone home. I began to despair. What would you feel like if grain from a whole field of corn was sent back and dumped in your yard?

But once again John came to our assistance, and he told us to send it down to Cronykeery and put it in his big garage where it would, at least, be dry. Next day, he went off to talk to his corn merchant and to my great relief this one accepted it, and took it away a day or two later. What I didn't know beforehand was that sprouted corn could be used for cattle feed, although of course it earned a bit less money.

After all that hassle there is still the grinding of the dried wheat into flour, and the making and the baking of the loaves. Finally they have to be distributed all over Ireland in small lorries and vans, so that people can buy fresh bread "baked today".

All of which has been going on since long before the feeding of the five thousand with only five little loaves and three fishes!

Kevin's Open Day

Last Sunday was Kevin's Open Day for families at Duffcarrig. Kevin is my grandson by marriage. He suffers from multiple handicaps.

He fell on his head when he was just learning to walk, with terrible consequences. This happened out in Australia, in 1966, where his father was working for an oil company. When I first met him, at about two years old, he could only lie on the ground and roll sideways! He had very little sight - we couldn't tell how much. His right side was very weak as it was partially paralysed. His left side was stronger but inclined to be spastic. His right leg didn't grow as much as the left, which means he has had to wear a calliper and a heavy built-up boot on his right foot. His speech was affected to start with although it has recovered almost entirely over time. He remains mildly mentally retarded, although he has special interests in which he is right up to the mark. For example, he is quite an expert at identifying bird-song, or pop music on the radio. He also remembers nearly all our important calender dates. The Camphill Communities are very strong at marking Saints' days, or special days such as family birthdays. They make the effort to connect these with the appropriate rituals, so Kevin always knows what's coming next and the dates and times thereof.

With such a catalogue of disabilities to cope with, one would expect Kevin to have developed into a miserable person. Thankfully, he is anything but! He is a most cheerful and happy character, who acknowledges his handicaps and loves to welcome you and to accept the help he needs. He falls over quite often, but picks himself up again quite cheerfully and carries on. We believe that he has a sort of "tunnel" vision which allows him to see some things he can focus on, but which doesn't allow him to see what's at his feet. He can distinguish between colours. I used to try him out by asking him to tell me the colour of each "Smarty" - his favourite sweets. He can swim quite adequately which is the best type of exercise for him. One summer, he was taken on a boating holiday by his community and he fell overboard into the Shannon! Someone rescued him and he seemed to think nothing of the incident.

Kevin is now in his thirties and, thankfully, he has never stopped making progress. He has lived in one or other of the Irish Camphill Communities for the last ten years or so. He is now in Duffcarrig, near Gorey, where they had the Open Day I want to tell you about. It was such a memorable day.

First, we gathered in the big hall which is new and beautiful, having only been completed a couple of years ago. Camphill Communities are special in many ways, one of which is their appreciation of beauty, be it in architecture, crafts, music or agriculture. So those parents or helpers who become involved often give their services for free. Duffcarrig is evidently rich in interesting architects. The last dwelling house to be built there prides itself in not having a straight wall anywhere!

We found Kevin in the hall with most of his fellow villagers and co-workers. We were welcomed by one of the co-workers who told us what was on offer. We were invited to a picnic lunch in the top field, where the midsummer bonfire was to be lit and later danced around to the strains of a very lively accordion. But before lunch we could go to see the various craft workshops, such as weaving, carpentry, pottery, cheese-making, and the new laundry. Alternatively, we could take part in a percussion band, or Eurythmics dancing, or visit the extensive gardens, or the farmyard where they milk some cows and have pigs and fowl. We chose to visit the pottery where Kevin goes to work every day.

Being limited to one active hand, Kevin can't do weaving or carpentry, but he can handle the china clay when damp. He made a pig as we watched, using a double mould. His younger brother, who was visiting with us, was delighted to discover that Kevin could help him to make a lamb in the same way.

Next came lunch in the cleared hayfield. It consisted of a big plateful of cold quiches and salads with sweets to follow and orange juice to drink. It was all home-made by the co-workers - a wonderful effort. The community is sixty strong before adding in the parents and families.

A sing-song then developed, followed by folk-dancing round the bonfire, which as it burned down we were encouraged to leap. I gathered this had something to do with defeating the Devil and any other evil spirits! Kevin and his mother went dancing while John and other visiting family members had plenty of space in which to play football.

Full of food and sunshine and happiness, we all gathered again in the hall where we were shown a slide show entitled "A day at Duffcarrig". This highlighted all the different jobs to be done by both "the villagers" and the co-workers. Kevin appeared at least three times and considered himself to be quite a star - we basked happily in reflected glory. We met and talked to many of the other parents and were able to connect each with their handicapped relation. Sadly, there were one or two unhappy people whose families hadn't been able to come. We all tried to include them in our conversations and to cheer them up.

We went for a tour of the gardens after this, and were amazed to come back to tea and homemade cakes and ice-cream for all. We were also given an opportunity to contact Kevin's co-worker about any personal problems. Finally there were "thank you" speeches and many goodbyes.

It was a wonderful day!

Bridie

Bridie died yesterday and I felt bereft. Suddenly the support which I had taken for granted for years was gone and I was forced to re-assess what Bridie had meant to me, especially with regard to the farming adventure we had shared together.

Bridie's death was not entirely unexpected. She had always been delicate and was often fighting off an infection. She was still fighting when we travelled down to Kilkenny to see her the previous week, and she managed to crack a joke or two and to give us a smile. She made me feel that my visit had significance for her as I arranged the flowers we had brought her from Ballinahinch. I can still see her eyes following me as I left her after saying my "goodbyes", and I felt it might be for the last time. I realised she was so weak after pneumonia that probably she wouldn't be able to pull up again, as she had done so often before.

And so it was. A week later the phone rang and her sister said 'Mrs. Tyner, this is Anna. Just to tell you that Bridie passed away this evening ....' and then her voice broke and she could say no more - dear kind Anna who had looked after her for so long.

My mother had two domestics - servants they were called in those days - and Lizzie, our cook, who had been with us since I was born, was Bridie's aunt. So when Mary, our parlour-maid, became ill and died very suddenly, Lizzie summoned her niece to come from the country to fill the gap. Bridie Lawlor had just turned nineteen, had never been out of Carlow before and was so nervous and shy that you could hardly hear her voice. But my mother took a great liking to her, and Bridie to my mother, so that she never left us until after my mother's death more than twenty five years later. During that time she not only cared for my mother in her loving way, but also nursed Lizzie who developed crippling arthritis in her old age.

Lizzie enjoys the sunshine at Ballinahinch (1968).

She also looked after my nephew, David, who came to spend his holidays with his Granny in Foxrock when his parents were in Ceylon. Bridie and he became good friends and she used to take him to the races at Leopardstown on her day off, or to the cinema on a wet day. He was quite a "handful" in those days, but Bridie seemed to have the secret of how to manage him. He stayed in touch with her even after he became a grandfather "down under" in Australia. As for herself, she never missed her "Bingo" night and liked to play cards as often as she could, down in the village hall.

I've described elsewhere how I came home from London and got the idea that I would like to farm. Lizzie and Bridie were thrilled and delighted with the idea. They were dying to get back to the country and to leave suburban, and rather snobbish, Foxrock. Also they knew how lonely and depressed my mother had been since we - my two brothers and I - were all away from home. They thought it would suit her too. So, when I went back to London to complete a series of puppet plays, the three of them began to look for a farm priced within our means. Against all expectations they found one - Ballinahinch.

I don't think I've ever given my mother sufficient credit for releasing Bridie and sending her to join me the minute we started farming. Of course, Bridie also represented my mother's interests, as my mother was building on the "granny flat". Naturally she wanted to assist me as much as she could, but if I hadn't had Bridie from the very outset I doubt that we would ever have farmed the land ourselves. I probably would have "set it" permanently to other people.

Bridie and my niece, Cherry, at Foxrock (1949).

I have always been good at planning and dreaming up crazy ideas like having an Irish breed of cows, such as the Kerries, but Bridie was good at putting these plans into action - sometimes even before I was really ready. In that instance, I hadn't even found out if there was a Kerry bull near enough to service our heifers! But once started, Bridie could keep things going day after day. If I had had to rise early every day, to feed the animals and do the milking, I would have become bored before long and would have planned something new. I was always like that from my earliest schooldays, where I was quick to pick up a subject but had forgotten all about it by next term. I have to admit that I took it for granted that Bridie would establish and stick to her routine as long as was needed, and she was happy to do just this. She would add her own particular colour, however, such as playing music for the cows to increase their yield. I was never sure if this worked. Perhaps they gave their milk more quickly to STOP her singing!

It never occurred to me to increase her salary or to give her more time off. Bridie, like Lizzie, had only one fortnight's holiday in the whole year to which she really looked forward. She would pack her suitcase weeks in advance, even making space for it under her pillow and sleeping on it! In addition, she would usually take a bundle of new rolls of wallpaper back home with her, and would paper one of her mother's rooms during her brief holiday. She took great pleasure in choosing and buying the wallpaper she thought her mother would like best. Of course, in those days she had to go home via Dublin, and the journey took the best part of a day. I'm sure that both Bridie and Lizzie thought they were much further away from their home than they actually were.

It was only after my mother's death that I found out what a small salary Bridie had been given over all the years she was with us. She told me then that she had never asked for a rise, as she feared that my mother would not be able to pay for Lizzie as well. She might have had to be sent home with no one to look after her. There did indeed come the time when Lizzie became so old and full of arthritis that even with the help of a wheelchair Bridie could no longer cope. I remember how shocked I was that Lizzie had to go into a County Council Old Age home, where she was kept in bed all the time.

To do myself justice, I always regarded Lizzie and Bridie as part of our family. I remember a time prior to all this - I think it was after my father had died - when we were considering building a new house. I planned having enough space to give each of them a good sized room to themselves. As it turned out, this would have made it too big and expensive and we had to give up the idea. So Lizzie and Bridie shared the one small bedroom for as long as I can remember. My mother used all the rest of the house for herself and her guests. True, the kitchen was theirs, and they had their own guests and friends visiting them there.

Now I'm glad to have my own warm kitchen to myself, but I feel sad when I realise that I'll never see the likes of Bridie and Lizzie again.

Miracles

Who would want miracles out of a book
When they're all around if you care to look?

There's a brilliant dandelion just over here
Its creator a consummate engineer.
The many-rayed face soaks up the sun
Then closes up tight - the magic's begun.
It opens a perfect ethereal sphere
Of tiniest parachutes - seeds poised to fly
As the very first breeze takes them floating by -
In such myriads many are sure to succeed
So that all good gardeners call it a weed.

Consider the hen, my own little hen,
Who lays me an egg for my tea, and then
The cock crows! It's at dawn that he crows
And wakens the world as everyone knows.
He struts the yard with high burnished tail
And scarlet cockscomb - a show-off male -
But after that he doesn't do much.
It's my hen that goes broody and lays her clutch
Of beautiful eggs. What is it that makes
Her keep them warm for as long as it takes
Fluffy chicks to emerge - peep out from her wings -
Where she keeps them safe from all harmful things?
Who wants to read of miracles then
When here in the yard is my little brown hen?

When you go fishing is it your wish
To pit your wits against that of the fish?
The beautiful fish clad in silver and gold,
The streamlined shape, the tales I am told
That the journey for home-coming salmon entails
The friendship of dolphins, the singing of whales
That our own brown trout are the loughs' great wealth
With my extra lung I can see for myself.
So who would choose torture from cruel hook
When Lough Corrib is there if you swim deep and look?

Have you looked at an in-calf cow head-on?
You'll find before calving she's broad as she's long.
At first I was worried, perhaps the vet for this cow?
'No, this is normal, he's not wanted now,
For she carries a load, a calf fully fashioned,
Expertly packed, protected and cushioned.
She'll find a quiet spot far from prying eyes -
She might drop her calf there before you arise.'
Next day she was slim with the calf at her side,
Strong on the special milk mother supplied.

Who would want miracles out of a book
When they're all around if you care to look.

"The Puddy" plans a trip, Wat's room, Ballinahinch (1992).

Index